D1099231

Walking Across

IRELAND

From Dublin Bay to Galway Bay

Michael Fewer is one of Ireland's top outdoors writers. He is the author of eleven books on walking, travel and countryside matters and has extensive knowledge of Irish topography, flora, fauna, archaeology and folklore. He has also written many magazine articles about walking and travel in Ireland and abroad. An architect with a particular interest in conservation, he works in the School of Architecture of the Dublin Institute of Technology.

To Teresa

WALKING ACROSS

IRELAND

From Dublin Bay to Galway Bay

MICHAEL FEWER

The Collins Press

Published in 2003 by
The Collins Press,
West Link Park,
Doughcloyne,
Wilton,
Cork

© Text Michael Fewer 2003
© Illustrations Michael Fewer

Michael Fewer has asserted his right to be identified as author of this work.

The material in this publication is protected by copyright law. Except as may be permitted by law, no part of the material may be reproduced (including by storage in a retrieval system) or transmitted in any form or by any means; adapted; rented or lent without the written permission of the copyright owners. Applications for permissions should be addressed to the publisher.

British Library Cataloguing in Publication data.

Fewer, Michael
    Walking across Ireland: from Dublin Bay to Galway Bay
    1. Fewer, Michael - Journeys - Ireland 2. Walking - Ireland
    3. Ireland - Description and travel
    I. Title
    914.1'704824

    ISBN 1903464390

Printed in Ireland by Woodprintcraft

Typesetting by The Collins Press

m160.216   914
            1704824

GALWAY COUNTY LIBRARIES

Contents

List of Illustrations

Introduction

In the 1970s British walker and writer, Alfred Wainwright, established a 306km (190 mile) walking route across Britain from the North Sea to the Irish Sea; it has since become a classic long distance path for walkers. Nearly ten years ago I set out to explore the possibility of such a route across the island of Ireland at its narrowest point with the intention of avoiding public roads as much as possible. The lack of cross-country footpaths and a footpath culture in the Irish countryside, an amenity which Britian has long enjoyed, made this a difficult task. I did, however, eventually put together a prototype route, and I wrote a description of it in *Walking World Ireland* magazine in 1995. Subsequently, through the advice of local people I had met on my first try and a little more research, I found that there were sections on which I could improve. *Walking From Dublin Bay to Galway Bay* is a narrative description of my experiences walking the final 290km (180 mile) route. Many of the earlier stages I carried out as day walks, availing of a drop-off in the morning and a pick-up in the evening, and the journey was carried out in three separate stages, in autumn, spring and summer. I have written elsewhere that pedestrian travellers, because of their mode of travel, have closer, more intimate contact with the places they pass through and the people they meet along the way than those who travel by any other means, and therefore experience a country in greater depth than those who travel by other means. The places I saw and the people I met, as I walked from the affluent suburbs of Dublin through the much forgotten and by-passed central lowlands to the vibrant Atlantic coast, gave me an unusual, cross-sectional view of Ireland at the beginning of the second millennium, at a time when Ireland was experiencing an unprecedented wave of prosperity that it was ill-prepared for.

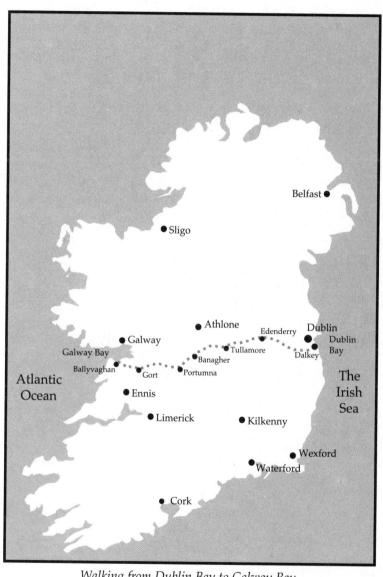

Walking from Dublin Bay to Galway Bay.
The route taken.

1

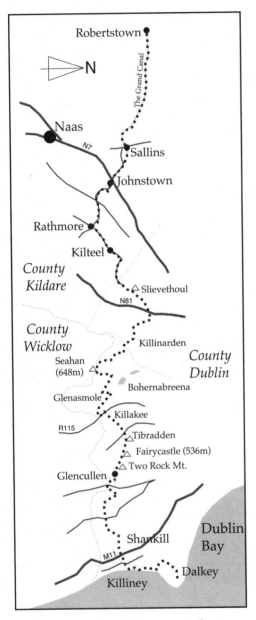

Robertstown

N

The Grand Canal

Naas

N7

Sallins

Johnstown

Rathmore

Kilteel

County
Kildare

△ Slievethoul

N81

County
Wicklow

Killinarden

Seahan
(648m) △

County
Dublin

Bohernabreena

Glenasmole

Killakee

R115

△Tibradden

△ Fairycastle (536m)

△ Two Rock Mt.

Glencullen

Dublin
Bay

Shankill

M11

Dalkey

Killiney

PART ONE

AUTUMN:
Dalkey
to
Robertstown

From Dalkey on Dublin Bay to Tibradden in the Dublin Mountains

O n my way up Green Road towards Dalkey village I turned to take a last look over Dublin Bay. A sea mist was slowly dispersing to reveal the silhouette of Dalkey Island with its Martello tower. Beyond a line of cormorant-clustered rocks that trailed northwards from the island, the blue-grey Hill of Howth materialised like a magic island at the far side of the bay, floating on a cloud of mist which obscured its southern shore. I took one last lingering look, and, turning away, continued inland, up the stone-walled laneway.

It was the beginning of the first stage of my walk to Galway Bay, which, to avoid the built-up areas of Dublin's suburbs, would take me on a long loop south of the outskirts

and into the foothills of the Dublin Mountains before I could begin to head west in earnest. I planned to finish my day's walking about 24km away at Edmondstown, on the fringe of the suburb of Rathfarnham.

Not far from the sea, in the grounds of a house called 'Nerano' is a two-and-a-half metre high statue of a man dressed in a colourful sailor's costume looking out over the sea. The figure was made in 1825, not from cast iron as one might expect, but concrete, and was one of the first examples of modern concrete work to be seen in Ireland. It was made by a firm called the MacAnespie Roman Cement Works at Great Brunswick Street, now called Pearse Street, in Dublin, and is a great piece of nineteenth-century enthusiasm, mounted on a bulbous plinth of granite bedrock. Dalkey, which developed from a miner's shanty town and is a glorious maze of houses and narrow roads, is as full of such visual delights as it is of homes with romantic names like 'Beacon Hill', 'Anno Santo', 'Hobbit Cottage' and 'Polly Villa', the Irish home of writer Maeve Binchy.

Winding streets lined with houses of every style and scale led me to Castle Street, the centre of Dalkey village. It is one of the few places in the Dublin area that has successfully retained its comfortable village atmosphere. There is a rich and balanced mix of inhabitants, old and young, affluent and not-so-affluent; building workers live next door to artists, and business people and bus drivers rub shoulders with writers and entertainers in the local butcher's shop. There is a supermarket, but it is of a reasonable size, which has allowed many small shops to survive and thrive. These, along with little cafés, a few good pubs and a couple of bookshops help maintain the scale and grain of the place.

The oldest evidence of human settlement here is the ruin

of St Begnet's church just off Castle Street, part of which is said to date back to the ninth century. I failed to find St Begnet listed as an official Irish saint, and remembered that the Catholic church some years ago had de-listed some Irish saints so maybe he was one of them. Eventually in an obscure journal I came across a suggestion that St Begnet, or St Bega or St Bees was 'a holy Irish virgin who had to flee to Cumberland. And there led the life of an anchoret ... she is remembered under 12 November and is styled *Virgo non Martyr'*.

Two fortified buildings the Norman period, Goat Castle and Archbold's Castle, give Castle Street its name. This was a busy place in Norman times when the area between Dalkey and Bullock Harbour had the name 'Port of the Seven Castles'. At the time Bullock Harbour was the only safe haven on the coast of Dublin Bay, and the town which grew up between it and the ancient Church of St Begnet took on considerable strategic importance. These two castles are what remain of seven which originally fortified the town walls.

Dalkey continued to be the most important port in the area until the end of the sixteenth century, when a harbour was developed at Ringsend which could take larger ships to serve the growing city of Dublin. By the middle of the seventeenth century it had become a ghost town with little more than a few dozen inhabitants, but in 1717, when the construction of what St John Joyce called 'one of the most remarkable and best breakwaters of its kind in the world' began at Ringsend, Dalkey was revived when the granite promontory south of the village became a major quarry for the building stone needed. Hundreds of stone masons, quarry workers and their families descended on Dalkey and made the place their home. The granite from Dalkey's quarry must have gained a high reputation, for hardly a decade passed subsequently during which the hill, ever decreasing in size, was not supplying stone for some great construction project.

On a monument in the grounds of St Begnet's Church, which stands on the north side of Castle Street, an event is recorded which led to the last great harvesting of stone from the quarry:

> Sacred to the Memory of the Soldiers belonging to His majesty's 18th Regiment of Foot, and a few belonging to other Corps, who, actuated by a desire of more extensive service nobly volunteered from the South Mayo and different Regiments of Irish militia of the Line, and who were unfortunately shipwrecked on the coast in the *Prince of Wales* Packet, and perished on the Night of 10th November, 1807. This tribute to their memory has been erected on their tomb by order of General the Earl of Harrington, commander of the Forces in Ireland.

The lives which were lost in the many previous wreckings in Dublin Bay, and particularly this disaster, led to the petitioning of the Lord Lieutenant to support the construction of a safe haven east of the sandbanks that surrounded the entry to the river Liffey. Close to the remains of a fort established by the fifth-century king Laoghaire, a site was chosen and in 1817 work began on the construction of Dun Laoghaire harbour. The harbour took 40 years to complete, during which Dalkey became an established village.

Except for a few early-risers, Dalkey had not yet woken up when I passed along Castle Street. I turned uphill beside Kent Terrace, a row of late Georgian houses with unusual iron-studded doors and strange decorative roof lights, and then up Dalkey Avenue, lined on both sides with a rich mix of late nineteenth-century houses.

At the top of Dalkey Avenue I turned onto a narrow footpath of rectangular granite slabs, barely resisting the encroachment of thick grass and weeds from each side. This is what remains today of what is locally called 'The Flags', a trackway built in the early nineteenth century for the purpose of bringing stone from Dalkey quarry down to Dun Laoghaire for the construction of the pier.

I emerged in the open again close to the entrance to Killiney Park. The houses here, close to the quarry, are laid out in haphazardly, with no apparent plan; a marvellous anti-order legacy reflecting the organic way in which the dwellings of the quarry workers, initially crude botháns, developed. This disorganised order, assisted by the rocky terrain of the original landscape, is what gives modern Dalkey and neighbouring Killiney a comfortable, informal ambience.

I made my way into the park and ascended towards the quarry, a ring of bare granite cliff-faces warmly reflecting the morning sun. There is little indication of how much of this hill has disappeared in the last 250 years, but the three-and-a-half-mile long wall at Ringsend, the one-and-a-half-mile long Dun Laoghaire piers, and the bridge over the Menai Straits in Wales must have taken, between them, a large share of Dalkey's granite hill.

In this age of manicured parks crossed by tarmac paths, the Dalkey side of Killiney Park is a refreshingly informal wilderness of gravelly tracks threading through clumps of gorse, brambles, buddleia and ash trees. There are occasional glimpses through the trees of the sheer and smooth cliffs of the old quarry reaching into the sky. As I left the trees and climbed towards the summit, a hazy Dublin Bay came into view behind. The final 100m to the summit, surmounted by a telegraph tower from the Napoleonic War, was by way of flights of steps, and the view at the top was most rewarding. I have stood on every high point in the greater Dublin area but I would vote this the finest viewpoint of all, particularly on a sunny morning. The sparkling Irish Sea stretched to the eastern horizon, while the incomparable Killiney Bay swept around south to terminate at rotund Bray Head. To the south-west, ranks of rounded Dublin and Wicklow Mountains faded into the haze. I could just pick out the rocky summit of Three Rock Mountain with its telecommunications gantry glistening in the morning sun, behind which lay my destination for the day. To the north west, at the foot of the Dublin hills, lay the city itself, transformed by distance and sunlight into a soft and colourful cityscape.

I followed the pathway towards the obelisk atop Killiney Hill south between great pillows of granite, each displaying striated scars left by the glacial ice-sheet. There are three monumental constructions on the summit of Killiney Hill or near it, the great obelisk, built by John Mapas in 1742 for the employment of the hungry poor after the harsh winter of that year, a smaller obelisk called Boucher's Monument, and a kind of ziggurat paved in mica schist.

Again I paused to take the view, and sat under the obelisk to identify landmarks on my route ahead for the day. Resembling, at a distance, an ancient round tower, the lead works chimney at Ballycorus, where I hoped to break the day and have lunch, was easy to spot. Behind it was an isolated dome-shaped outcrop called Carrick Golligan, one of the family of eroded quartzite tors that include Bray Head and the two Sugarloafs to its south and east; my route would take me around the north side of it.

I descended steeply through the park and out onto the

public roadway, passing through an ornate castellated gateway which was at one time the gate into the Killiney Castle demesne. I was enjoying the warmth of the morning as I walked through opulent suburbia. Stands of Scots pines and eucalyptus cast deep pools of shade which contrasted sharply with the floods of bright sunlight between, and when the silvered sea came into view below, one could easily mistake the place for the French or Italian Riviera.

The way down onto Killiney Strand was a narrow, steep and stepped passageway. It was a pleasant route I had taken before, overhung with virginia creeper and flowering shrubs, and I left the road to follow it.

I continued downhill, and within a minute could hear the swish of waves breaking on the pebbles of Killiney beach. Passing under a railway bridge I emerged from the shade into brilliant sunlight and onto the long curving beach, stretching away for three shingly miles towards Bray.

Although I was now walking on the level for the first time since I had left Dalkey village, my feet sank deep into the stoney beach with each step and it was slow going. It was nearly 10am now and was warming up well, so I stopped to remove my pullover and sit a while to enjoy the scene. The beach was deserted but for two foreign-looking girls cooking breakfast at the mouth of a tent pitched under the cliffs, while another walked along the water's edge collecting pretty pebbles. The pebbles and stones on Killiney beach are mostly composed of limestone; the nearest limestone bedrock is at Blackrock, five miles away, but geologists suggest that the pebbles also come from much further away, ferried by Ice Age glaciers tens of thousands of years ago. Without searching too hard, you can also find fragments of a pink-purple granite, which is only found in rock form on Ailsa Craig, the dome-like island off the Scottish coast, at the entry to the Firth of Clyde.

Soon I was on my way again; I had no way of knowing what kind of detours or obstacles would hold me up along the way, and I was anxious to get to Glencullen before 6pm. Towards the southern end of the beach I passed through a wilderness of bamboo grass, daisies, yarrow and thistles, fussed over by a flock of goldfinches. Perched atop thistles, the birds were plucking the seeds out of the heads, each pluck releasing a small cloud of silky seed parasols that gleamed in the sunlight like puffs of white smoke.

A few minutes later I reached a concrete staircase up the cliffside, which took me abruptly out of the seashore world into a leafy suburbia. The splashing of waves quickly faded to be replaced by peace as I entered a shady laneway leading uphill. After over an hour of heading south as my route dictated, it was a relief to have finally turned west towards the Atlantic coast of Ireland, even if it was still over 170 miles away.

Crossing a busy main road, I found myself in a neighbourhood of tiny cottages and bungalows with names like Hawthorn Cottage and The Nook. In the midst of these, with a roof in the same terracotta tiles as the cottages, was a beautiful public library, its weathervaned tower and gently imposing doorway giving it a slightly grander scale than its dwelling-house neighbours. It is one of about 80 libraries in Ireland which were built early in the twentieth century with the financial assistance of the railroad millionaire, Andrew Carnegie; this little jewel was designed by the architect R.M. Butler and built about 1912.

I soon found myself in the country; sleek, well-bred horses grazed in roadside fields surrounded by tall deciduous

trees, and here and there glimpses could be had of large comfortable-looking houses well set back from the road. Ahead I
could see Three Rock Mountain rising rounded and sunlit,
and to its left, identified by the tall stone chimney on its summit, Ballycorus Hill, where I had promised myself a break.

At a crossroads I came to Rathmichael Church, a rounded nineteenth-century granite building with steep roofs. It
was designed by Deane and Woodward, architects of Trinity
College Geology Department among other buildings in
Dublin, and whose work is often recognised by the strong use
of Celtic Revival motifs beautifully carved in stone. A little
further on I turned onto a narrow boreen, which seemed to
disappear into bushes after a short distance. In front of the
bushes stood a small and weathered granite crucifix behind
which a barely discernable grassy path continued into the
trees; if you did not know it was there you would miss it. I
crouched low and squeezed my way through the thorns to
find myself on Rathmichael Lane, an early Christian roadway leading to Rathmichael Monastery, some of the ruins of
which can be found further on. It had changed little since the
time I had found it some years before, a tunnel of foliage over
an old roadbed of worn cobbles. In early Christian times
monks led burdened pack mules along it, travelling to or
from Glendalough.

Soon I left the ancient road to strike out west again,
uphill into a wood. Rabbits grazing on the pathway ahead of
me scurried for the dark safety of the thorns as I approached,
and disturbed wood pigeons blundered their way noisily out
of the trees. I was passing through a small piece of forestry
which appeared to have been forgotten, and was in the
process of returning to primeval wildwood. Thistles and rag-
weed competed for cleared ground, while the base of the odd

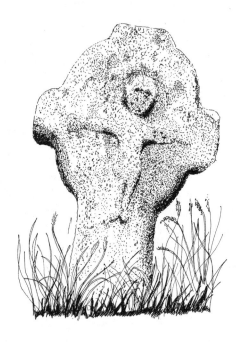

remaining tree was obscured with great clumps of bramble festooned with woodbine. It was nearly three hours since I had set out, and as noon approached, the sun's warmth, combined with the steady climbing, had given me a thirst. In a quiet glade I found a suitable tree-trunk to sit on while I took a short break to have a drink and review my progress.

I climbed westwards, crossed a public road, and entered another wood. The trees threw a pleasant cooling shade over the path as I climbed, while extensive views opened up behind me of Bray Head and the Irish Sea beyond, rewards for my exertions. A man coming down told me the top was a 'fair bit off', so I was pleasantly surprised when a few minutes later I saw the stone chimney on the summit of Ballycorus only a few hundred metres ahead.

The 22m-high chimney was built early in the nineteenth century as a flue to discharge the poisonous gases from the lead-smelting works on the north-west side of the hill. A stone tunnel built to carry the fumes to the chimney from the smelter about a mile downhill is still in existence although in ruined condition. The galena, or lead ore, processed here at Ballycorus was originally mined locally but when the veins were exhausted, the plant continued to smelt ore from the mines at Glendalough in County Wicklow. Most of the refined lead was made into ingots and exported but some was used to manufacture musket shot, which was made by dropping measured amounts of molten lead from a height into water; by the time the lead reached the water, it had solidified into as near a perfect sphere as it was possible to manufacture at the time.

I reached the chimney to find a middle-aged man and woman sitting on a rock nearby eating sandwiches. As I unslung my rucksack I greeted them and they both smiled and wished me good day.

'Will you join us?' the man asked with an Irish accent trimmed with an English inflection, as he saw me take out my food.

I said I'd be delighted, and settling myself on a rock beside them, dug my sandwiches out of my rucksack. We chatted about the weather, of course, and how it looked like being warm later in the day.

Closer now, I could see that they were not the sort of people who make a habit of climbing hills; both were quite red-faced from their exertions, and while he was wearing runners, she had sandles on which were unsuitable for walking.

As we talked, the reason for their presence at the chimney became clear. They were both born in Shankill but had spent most of their adult lives in Manchester. Home on holiday, and celebrating their thirtieth wedding anniversary, they decided to climb to the chimney, where he had proposed to her 32 years previously. They had not realised how tough they would find the climb but they made it, huffing and puffing, and were thrilled to be there. They had prospered in England and planned to return to Ireland when he retired in a couple of years.

'It doesn't look like we will be able to now, however,' she told me.

'Although we have a lot saved, and our house in Manchester will fetch good money, it's nothing compared to the prices here. We would have little savings left to enjoy life.'

He said they had lots of Irish friends in Manchester with a similar problem, people who had worked all their lives with the dream of returning home on retirement, but Ireland's new-found prosperity was making that dream impossible.

'Anyway, it's not the same,' she said. 'I suppose the home

you dream about is like the way it was when you knew it, except in your dream your circumstances have changed, you have lots of money! There was no work when we left and things were simpler. Now everybody has money and jobs, it's really a different place, so maybe we're better off at home in Manchester.'

They offered me biscuits and I shared my mandarin oranges with them. When we were finished they struggled to their feet, not relishing the trek down again. They were surprised when I told them where I was heading for and where I had come from, and I got the impression they thought I was a bit mad. I slung my rucksack on my back again and wishing them 'Happy Anniversary,' I set off towards the trees again. As I looked back, they had their arms around each other and were watching me go.

The long, low form of Two Rock Mountain, my next destination, was taking on shape and detail ahead. Before it were three thickly wooded hills I would have to cross to reach it, and according to my map there were convenient forestry tracks and paths that I could use. Entering the trees on the first of these hills I found a well-made rustic timber sign that warned of theft from cars, urging you to bring all your valuables with you, and forbidding horseriding. As I ascended the pathway, I saw that at least the last instruction was not being obeyed; the peaty soil of the path was churned up by countless hoofs into a morass that after wet weather would make it almost impassable.

Leaving the path I headed more directly uphill through an area of well-spaced trees, many of which had been blown flat but had resumed growth, resulting in a strange forest of twisted, tortured tree trunks, between which domes of bare granite protruded from a rusty brown carpet of pine needles.

Beyond the highest point of the hill, a rock garden of heather, gorse and bracken, I descended a pathway steeply westwards through a sun-dappled woodland, my boots crunching satisfyingly on dried-out leaves and twigs. The path led me onto the Dublin to Enniskerry road, which follows a deep and dramatic north-to-south cleft in a granite hill called the Scalp, its steep sides overhung with precarious-looking boulders. The place has been the subject of tourist curiosity for a couple of hundred years, and referred to in nineteenth-century travel guides as 'a tremendous chasm', 'prodigious disjointed masses of stone' and a 'frightful channel'. I had climbed almost vertically down it with a friend a few years previously but this time was going to depend on an old boreen which I had found on my previous journey, hoping it was still there.

At the roadside there was a country petrol station with shop attached, the first I had seen since leaving Dalkey. Secluded beyond the shop I found the boreen I was looking for. I followed it behind a couple of houses and almost immediately ascended steeply beside an old demesne wall, a little stream trickling down at its side. After a short distance the boreen became overgrown, and I had to hack my way through stands of tall healthy nettles. I was beginning to think I would have to retrace my steps and find another way over the hill when, suddenly, the nettles came to an end and I crossed a low wall out into the open once again.

I found myself beside the great artificial ski-slope of the Dublin Sports Hotel and I followed the edge of a wood southwards up along the ski run, and into a field recently planted with young conifers. I headed westwards again through ankle-threatening rough ground, covered with a dense forest of the summer's dried-out foxgloves. As I waded through the overgrown field the noise of my passage was added to by other sounds. Disturbed by my presence, unseen and therefore unidentified creatures scurried and rustled through the tangled grass ahead of me as I walked. They were clearly large animals, certainly big enough to be rats, but I hoped they were only rabbits. In the fifteen minutes I spent crossing the field none showed itself, and I was very relieved to reach a track and get away from the mysterious creatures.

I now had to detour considerably around Ballybetagh bog, a broad low-lying depression which was once a postglacial lake. I followed the track westwards past a bungalow from which issued two loudly barking, scraggy mongrels. Steeling myself for attack and gripping my stick tightly, I was relieved when it became apparent that their barks were worse than their potential bites. They stayed within their own territory, behind some invisible line, howling and growling at me as I passed. A little further along I came to a gate across the track, and as I carefully closed it behind me, I saw it carried a sign, facing the other direction, which said 'No Trespassing'!

The name of the area I was passing through, Ballybetagh, dates back to pre-Norman Ireland, and refers to an unusual Irish custom. Hospitality and generosity were virtues which were highly esteemed in ancient Ireland. This was acknowledged by the Brehon laws, in which a person of rank could be excused for shortcomings like deficiency of food or drink, at the unexpected arrival of a large number of guests, or the failure of a tributary chief to supply food he was obliged to. The laws also laid down that a chieftain must entertain a guest without asking questions, so the guest's name, business and where he was from might not be known. An outward expression of this custom was the establishment of *brugha*, or free public hostels, by a chieftain along the roads in his territory, where travellers and officials could expect to be accommodated. One type of free inn was run by a *biatach*, or *betagh*, who was given a large tract of land free of rent, about 1,000 acres, to enable him to carry out his responsibilities. Ballybetagh, the town of the *betagh*, must have been the site of one of these free inns.

In minutes, I was on a public road again and heading north. According to the map, in the previous twenty minutes I had left County Dublin, entered County Wicklow and then returned into County Dublin. To my left the fields fell away towards Ballybetagh bog, while ahead the road ascended towards a hill and small wood. Extensive scientific studies of the soils under the bog here were carried out in the 1930s, involving the retrieval of soil samples from deep in the ground, and in places, the opening of large trenches exposing ground that had not seen the light of day for 10,000 years. The material found, including remains of animals, plants and microscopic pollen grains, provided a graphic picture of what it was like here at Ballybetagh shortly after the glaciers of the Great Ice Age had finally receded northwards. The finds told of a tundra landscape of shallow lakes left behind by the ice, interspersed with copses of small trees such as juniper, birch and willow. On the banks of one of these lakes, what is now Ballybetagh bog, herds of moose, reindeer and *Megaloceros giganteus*, the extinct Irish giant deer, gathered in wintertime. The moose is a big animal, but the giant deer would have towered over him, standing 2m high at the shoulder, his head crowned with dangerous-looking, but in reality, fragile antlers with a span of almost 4m. Compared to the Lilliputian species we would know in Ireland today, this animal, which roamed the land in great herds, must have been something truly spectacular.

914
1704824

The *Dublin Penny Journal* of 1834, one of the earliest Irish periodicals to take an interest in the mysteries of the past, devoted much space to 'the fossil deer'.

M160,216

When and where did this gigantic species of deer exist? Such is the question which arises at once to every man's mind – yet nothing but mere conjecture can be given in reply. No tradition of its actual existence remains; yet so frequently are bones and antlers of enormous size dug up in various parts of the island that the peasantry are acquainted with them as the 'old deer' and in some places these remains are so numerous and so frequent that they are often thrown aside as useless lumber. A pair of these antlers were used as a field gate near Tipperary. Another pair had been used for a similar purpose near Newcastle, County Wicklow, until they were decomposed by the action of the weather. There was also a specimen in Charlemont House, the town residence of the Earl of Charlemont, which is said to have been used for some time as a temporary bridge across a rivulet in the County Tyrone ... similar remains have been found in Yorkshire, Essex, the Isle of Man, Germany, near Paris and in Lombardy.

GALWAY COUNTY LIBRARIES

During the excavations here at Ballybetagh 100 years later, the remains of numerous giant deer, all males, were found in a relatively small area. The late Professor Frank Mitchell suggested that because the male deer exhausted themselves during the annual rutting season, they began the winter, when grazing was in shorter supply, in poor condition and vulnerable to severe weather conditions. About 11,000 years ago a prolonged period of severely cold weather, almost a return to Arctic conditions, occurred, which may have finished off the Ballybetagh herds, and subsequently all the giant deer in Ireland, although it is thought that the species did not become completely extinct in the remote parts of the Middle East and Asia until some hundreds of years ago.

The afternoon sun was becoming hot as I left Ballybetagh and began to climb towards Glencullen, one of County Dublin's prettiest villages, a very pleasant scatter of old and new cottages with a library, school and church. As I climbed gently into the village, I passed a granite-built cottage called 'The Arsenal', the home of the late Billy Cannon, stonemason, music lover and walker, and his wife Maisie. He had never known Ireland's doyen of walkers, J.B. Malone but had got so much pleasure following the man's walking guides that after Malone's death in the early 1990s he carved a stone memorial to him which can be seen on the Wicklow Way above Lough Tay. I asked him once why he named his house the Arsenal, and he replied 'I have a big family; what would you call a building full of cannons?'

It was very hot and I was attracted into the shade of the old Glencullen churchyard to sit down for a drink of water. I tried to make a sun-hat from my handkerchief to keep the sweat from my eyes. I stopped to explore the remains of an old church set in a shady graveyard. A plaque on the roofless ruin said that it had been erected 'to the honour and glory of God' in 1824, and it was clearly once a building of considerable character in the perpendicular style.

Back on the road again, I passed the fine little Carnegie library which Glencullen has enjoyed since 1907. One of the innovations incorporated when it was built was the provision of lavatory basins in the cloakroom so that readers could wash their hands before handling the books. A little farther

on was the 'new' church, built about a year after the library, and Johnny Foxe's pub. Foxes, at 918 feet above sea level, is signposted as the highest pub in Ireland and has been much extended in recent years. It is decorated in the 'Irish olde worlde' style, with low ceilings, dark-panelled walls decorated with old-fashioned advertisements, and shelves of old books, clay jars and other curiosities. It is an enormously popular tourist venue, and is always packed to the doors in summertime, which must leave the locals without a pub.

A short distance to the south, nestled in trees is Glencullen Lodge, an elegant villa of the early nineteenth century, fronting a much older house that was for many years the property of Fitzsimons family. In the mid-nineteenth century one of the Fitzsimons married Ellen, daughter of Daniel O'Connell, the Liberator, and he often used visit Glencullen; one of his 'Monster Meetings' which used to attract large concourses of people was held further up the valley in a natural amphitheatre in 1845. Meetings of the Catholic Association were held in the house, and the Bill for Catholic Emancipation is said to have been drafted there, on a table which is still in the hands of the Fitzsimons family. In 1914 the poet Joseph Campbell lived there, and in the 1920s the novelist Francis Stuart and his wife Iseult, the daughter of Maud Gonne MacBride, stayed there for a while.

Leaving Glencullen behind, I left the road after a few minutes and made my way into the woods that cover the eastern slopes of Two Rock Mountain. I left the track briefly to have a look at the megalithic tomb that stands in a clearing in the wood. It is an elaborate arrangement of granite slabs making up what the archaeologists call a wedge-shaped gallery grave. There are 200 or 300 similar religious or funerary monuments to be found around Ireland, built about

4,000 years ago. The cremated remains were poured into decorative clay urns, which were placed in three compartments or enclosures, originally capped with flat slabs of stone, and the whole construction was covered with a mound of earth. It was not easy to imagine how this place looked when the Bronze-Age people gathered to bury their dead but the ambience and the juxtaposition of the granite boulders spoke volumes, and rendered redundant the terse description of the site on a nearby rusty sign.

Leaving the trees behind, I headed steeply uphill again for the local summit, less than imaginatively called Two Rock, after the two granite tors that are the only features on this heather-covered hill. Flies buzzed densely around my head and I had to pluck a frond of bracken to keep them at bay. The warmth of the sunlit air was beginning to undergo a welcome wane now as altitude was gained, and I felt a hint of a westerly breeze on my damp forehead. As I climbed, the peaks of the Dublin Mountains and those of north Wicklow came into sight to the south, layer upon layer of them in a series of hazy blue shades. Kippure, County Dublin's highest, is always easy to identify due to its tall television mast, and it is then easy to pick out Maulin, Djouce and Mullacleevaun.

From Three Rock I turned north towards the highest point of the hill, a Bronze Age cairn called the Fairy Castle. It is a place where I walk frequently because it is close to home, and at any time other than Sunday, it tends to be deserted. The only encounters I usually have on this hill are deer, ravens and grouse but as I got to the Fairy Castle a man was sitting on the top of the cairn with four young boys. He was from Crumlin, a Dublin suburb, and he introduced me to his four sons, ranging in age from five-year-old James, through John and Dennis to Sean at eleven. They were coming to the end of a day in the mountains, and running dangerously low on lemonade, the last of which Sean husbanded in a large plastic bottle. The boys told me that their father got them up very early on weekend mornings, and after they make their picnic they get a bus into town to catch another to the mountains. They walk a route that their father had reconnoitred a few days before and return home again by bus. They were wonderfully enthusiastic, indicating all the nearby peaks they had climbed, and Sean recited their names,

'The Sugarloaf, Kippure, Maulin, Kilmashogue and Tibradden – that means 'the house of Bradden'. Taken aback at this information and the importance he put on it, I asked him what Kilmashogue meant. With a quick glance at his father, who looked on approvingly, he said,

'The church of Mashoge. He was a saint in the olden days.'

Their father told me that although he is not a Gaelic speaker, he likes to find out the meaning of names and he discusses them with the boys as they walk, to put some personality on the places they go to.

I would have liked to talk further but I needed to be on my way, so I left the tired but happy bunch and headed down along a boggy saddle towards Tibradden. The moorland around me was bright with bursts of purple and yellow, produced by heather and gorse, which was blossoming for the second time in the year. The sun still shone but an evening haze was settling a blue filter on the hills, and the air was becoming cooler. My hip joints and my legs were beginning to feel a little stiff as I ascended the gentle slope of Tibradden ridge but generally I was in good shape.

Passing the confusion of glacial erratics that litter the ridge, I reached the highest point and sat beside the ruined passage grave there to drink the last of my liquid supplies, a sachet of orange juice. To the west on the far side of the valley, dark Glendhu and Cruagh Mountain loomed, already in shade as the sun was sinking. Ahead, the great flat spread of Dublin city was in view again, while to the east, Kelly's Glen and Kilmashogue Mountain shone in the sunlight. Recent investigations have revealed a network of neolithic field walls protruding from the peat on Kilmashogue. I was surprised to see from where I sat that some of these were clearly visible as dotted lines of granite stones glistening white and reflecting the low sun. I say surprised, because I had sat in this same place many times looking over the same view without noticing these walls, and now that I knew they were there, they seemed perfectly obvious.

The top of the cairn and the roof of the passage grave where I sat was missing, so the monument could be seen in plan. The destruction of the rest occurred in the early nineteenth century when the tomb was excavated by a local landlord and his gamekeeper. Their main interest seemed to be the treasure that might be contained in the burial chamber, and since no detailed records were kept, we must assume that the structure was originally a dome-shape of corbelled stones and covered by a mound of stones. It is amazing how neat the surviving courses of stones making up the chamber sides are, even after thousands of years, although in the twenty years since I had seen this monument for the first time, it has deteriorated, probably from the numbers of walkers using it as a picnic place.

I thought about the Crumlin man and his boys and their interest in the names of places. In Ireland we have a rich heritage of placenames, although as we move into the cyber age the knowledge and interest in such things seems to be dying

fast. And what a pity that would be, especially for those who love the countryside in all its facets.

Every prominent rock, every tiny valley, each and every field and old boreen in this land has a name. And although ancient, in most cases their meaning is still clear and relevant for walkers today. The name Tonlegee in Wicklow means the 'backside of the wind' and suggests what it can frequently be like there, while Knockatillane (from *sillean*, dripping) in the same county suggests a wet, boggy hill. Coumnageeha in south Tipperary, which means the valley of the wind, can suggest to a walker what to expect there.

Even aspects of the landscape now long gone can be suggested by a placename. In my home place I often pass a field called *Pairc an Seana-Shraid*, the field of the old village, so once there must have been a settlement there. The northern ridge of the Comeragh Mountains is called *Knockanaffrin*, or the hill of the Mass. While the eastern slopes are precipitous, the west sweeps off gently westwards towards the Nire valley, and one can easily imagine, in penal times, it being a safe place to bring the peasants together to celebrate an illegal mass. One often comes across places with names like *Cnocaniller* and *Aill na gCat*, which recall the time not so long ago when eagles and wild cats were still to be found in Ireland. The knowing of these stories, lightly concealed in our placenames, adds a few extra jigsaw pieces to the landscape mystery, and certainly adds to a walker's pleasure.

I started downhill for the last time that day, disturbing a cloud of peacock butterflies as I entered the trees. As I reached a forestry car park, I was suddenly surrounded by indications that I had left the true countryside behind and had come within the influence of a city. The ground was scattered with sweet papers, broken glass and condom packets, and standing wheel-less on the littered tarmac was an obviously stolen and pillaged car, its owner's personal belongings strewn around it.

A mile down the road at Edmondstown I found Doherty's pub, and hauled myself inside to refresh myself with a cool pint of Guinness.

From Tibradden to Kilteel,
County Kildare

The following morning I was at Tibradden again to start the second stage of my journey. My goal for the day was the village of Kilteel, on the western side of the mountains and just over the county border in Kildare. Between Cruagh and Kilteel I would follow a long, winding route that would take me over two mountains, across three valleys and over a series of foothills before I would see the plains of Kildare stretching westwards.

From the bridge at Tibradden I headed south following a mountain stream which tumbled and cascaded below me in a frantic rush north that would eventually bring its peat-stained waters into the heart of Dublin city before reaching the Liffey and Dublin Bay.

The sun strained to cut through a misty morning haze as I followed a forestry road up Cruagh Mountain, my initial progress slow as I zig-zagged steeply up the mountainside, shaking off a good nights' sleep. Nothing stirred at this early hour, even the birds were quiet, but scattered on the track I saw the fresh prints and steaming droppings of a small herd of deer which had probably just moved into the trees as I approached. As I ascended, the city was gradually revealed below, stretching northwards into haze.

When the track levelled out at about 1,400 feet I sought and found a rough pathway leading off to the left and climbing westwards through black, soggy peat. I followed the path uphill through trees which began to thin out as I neared the western edge of Cruagh wood. A flock of goldcrests came chirping and swooping through the air towards me, and alighted in the top of a nearby conifer. They were constantly on the move, their tiny green bodies hanging upside down, looking like strange, animated fruit, as they foraged for caterpillar morsels among the pine needles.

Below, through the now sparse trees at the edge of the forest, I could see a deep ravine descending towards the east, a landmark that allowed me to confirm my position on the map, indicating that I was a little further south than I had intended but heading in the right direction. As I left the last of the trees behind and strode out through a ground-hugging yellow sea of late gorse onto the open plateau, the ridge of Tibradden came into sight behind, and beyond it the mound of the Fairy Castle. The featureless moor of Killakee stretched out ahead of me to the west, disappearing into a bank of low, early morning cloud, with the higher ground of Glendhu Mountain filling the horizon to the south.

I found a path heading roughly westwards and set off to follow it. As I progressed, the bank of cloud ahead partially lifted, revealing a very flat stretch of moorland with few features other than scattered clumps of gorse and a few fence posts. This moor, being close to my home, is for me a frequent place of resort when seeking quietness and the bracing mountain air. Although I have crossed it many times I have probably, due to lack of any real landmarks, never followed the same route, and would only know roughly where I was at any particular point. It is easy, even for the most experienced, to become completely disorientated walking in cloud on a mountain. Even if one is familiar with the area, and is using a map and compass, distance can be difficult to judge. Landmarks that should be familiar can be rendered unrecognisable when viewed only partially and from unfamiliar angles.

A half-mile away I identified the highest point of Cruagh Mountain marked by a tiny cairn and a pole. I was glad to see that I was on the correct bearing to pass across the plateau between Killakee and Glendhu to reach the public road above Glenasmole. Another opening in the cloud base to the north revealed the bare stone hulk of the Hellfire Club on Montpelier Hill to the north west, further confirming my position.

Soon I came to a change in level in the ground, and clambered down 1.5m of peat to meet a familiar old bog road that would take me the rest of the way across the plateau. It was good to get into my stride on the granite gravel, and I felt I was now really on my way. I had walked this lonely, isolated road many times, escaping from the city below. The nineteenth-century mountaineer, A.F. Mummery, wrote of such walking:

The troubles and cares of life, together with the essential vulgarity of a plutocratic society, are left far below – foul miasmas that cling to the lowest bottoms of reeking valleys. Above, in the clear air and searching sunlight, we are afoot with the quiet gods, and men can know each other and themselves for what they are …

One does not even require 'good' weather to enjoy the peace mountains can bring. When the weather is bad and one has to battle against cold driving rain and wind, the sense of jousting with the elements is also a strong and satisfying one; when one has escaped from long, self-inflicted hours of these conditions and sits in the warmth of a pub fireplace with a drink, the euphoria experienced can be very special. Another man of the nineteenth century, poet and artist William Morris, wrote:

Indeed I am waxen weary: but who heedeth weariness, that hath been day-long on the mountain in the winter weather's stress?

I was suddenly jolted out of my reverie as a snipe burst out of cover a yard ahead of me, and went jinking off into the distance; I was amused to find the shock of it gave me goose-pimples! Near here I once came close to observing a falcon 'stooping' on its prey.

I had followed the old turf road, glittering with flakes of mica, uphill towards the sun, and I had not gone far before a grouse took off from the heather in front of me, flying furiously for cover with bursts of wingbeats and intermittent short glides, cackling all the way. Probably due to the sun in my eyes, I did not see what happened next. There was a strange sound and a burst of activity in the heather ahead. I left the track and crossed the heath. As I approached, two large birds of prey rose together into the air. They looked muscular and bulky as they took off, and I realised they were peregrines. They gained height with fast wingbeats, and the lead bird interrupted its climb briefly with a sudden and incredibly fast plummetting dive to join the second bird, the sun catching their white breasts. They had dark tails but their upper plumage, only glimpsed as they had taken off, was brownish rather than slate grey, which suggested they were juveniles. Rising on the breeze in an astonishingly fast climb, they levelled out and, pausing their fast wingbeats for short spurts of glide, they circled around me, rising all the time, until they passed right over my head and flew away. In seconds they were gone over the horizon.

I wondered why they had been in the heather where there is little cover until they must have had a kill. I headed over to the spot from where they had taken off, a male red grouse, more or less intact, lay in the heather. As I reached it the bird leapt up and blundered off a few yards with that familiar cackle – it was still alive!

I approached again, and it made another attempt to escape, leaping and half flying away a few yards, only to tumble head over heels in a clump of heather. The grouse was panicky and trembling, looking quite bedraggled, the feathers on his neck askew, and his wing feathers twisted. But he got up again and this time flew a bit farther before crash-landing. It seemed he was still stunned, but was recovering, and each time he launched himself he did better. I decided to leave him be – I thought he might survive his ordeal if he rested up a while – so I strode off back to the path and continued on my way. Usually a peregrine's prey is killed instantly on impact in the air, but this grouse had survived the initial stoop; the peregrines were a pair of young, inexperienced birds, attacking prey a lot bigger than usual, and they did not do it well.

A minute later the sun broke free of its enveloping cloud and shone warmly over the moor, brightening the sombre colours and reflecting brilliantly off the many ponds and pools. An expanding patch of blue sky completed the change.

The high moorland plateau I was crossing has long been known as the Featherbeds, a name that harks back to the time before widespread harvesting of turf began and the bog here was in summertime, a shimmering white carpet of bog cotton. Up to recent years it was a busy place in summer and autumn, as many Dublin families cut, stacked, gathered and bagged turf for their winter fires. It was cheap fuel, and although the harvesting was labour intensive, family members young and old formed life-long bonds, and great inter-family friendships were born, as the annual outings for turf-cutting became a tradition that spanned through the years of the early and mid-twentieth century. Only in the last decade has the tradition died, and now very few spend summer evenings on the Featherbeds cutting turf.

Recently I had the good fortune to meet one of the last turf-cutters. On yet another lone traverse of Killakee I was making my way through disused turf cuttings when I spotted a man sitting in the doorway of a bothan made of peat sods built into a turf bank, the whole thing almost invisible except for the doorway itself. I went over to say hallo. A bespectacled man in his late sixties, he was wearing an old gaberdine coat over an even older pin-striped suit, the trousers of which were tucked into wellington boots. He asked if I was having a good walk, and invited me to sit in out of the chill breeze. As he talked he was meticulously organising a cup of tea with milk and plenty of sugar for himself from a flask, and he offered me a cup.

We chatted about turf cutting and he told me that the numbers had dropped off terribly in recent years. He remembered a time when as many as 700 people, men women and children, were out on the bog every good summer's evening;

now he thought there were about a dozen turf-cutters left.

'When the gas came in the 1970s, that was the end of the turf. I suppose there was a bit of affluence around then also, and the idea of having Kinsale gas to your door must have been tempting, particularly for those whose youngsters were no longer interested in hard work on the bog.'

He told me he found the peace of the bogs and the work a wonderful restorative; he had been a bar manager in Dublin, and when things were really stressful he would repair up here to the relaxing rhythm of slicing with the slean, lifting and throwing the sod. He took down a slean that had been hanging on the wall of the bothan.

'It belonged to my father and his father before him, and dug many a Kerry sod of turf in the old days,' he said. 'It's well over 100 years old.'

He also showed me a broad, sword-like blade, resembling the kind of hay-knife usually used for notching vertical cuts in the turf.

'My grandfather used this all his life; it was once a harpoon for catching basking sharks that he got off a Mayo fisherman.'

He complained that he could no longer leave tools in his little bothán; it had been broken into a number of times and tools had been stolen by 'gurriers that come up from the city'.

When I finished my tea I continued on my ramble, leaving him sitting in his doorway enjoying a pipe in the evening sun. Some months later when I passed I found the bothán abandoned and roofless.

As the bog road began to descend, the dark shape of a mountain emerged from the mist to the west, its southern parts concealed by a sharp-edged curtain of dark grey fog rising out of the valley of Glenasmole. I was relieved a few minutes later to find that my instinctive navigation had been accurate when I reached the Military Road and turned to follow it south. Now used mainly as a scenic route to Glendalough, this road was built in the early years of the nineteenth century to allow the British army swift access deep into mountainous Wicklow, where for centuries Irish dissidents and rebels had successfully avoided apprehension. As far back as the fourteenth century the clans of Wicklow had been a thorn in the side of the English rulers; even as late as 1800, rebel bands led by the legendary Michael Dwyer and the self-styled General Holt, operating from mountain hideouts on the very doorstep of Dublin, continued the abortive rebellion of 1798 by carrying out raids on loyalist settlers on the borders of Dublin and Wicklow. To finally address this problem, and to ensure that Wicklow would never again be a rebel refuge, this great road, stretching through the middle of the mountains all the way to Aghavannagh, 40 miles to the south, and a number of barracks along its route, were built, and the asylum of the Wicklow Mountains became a thing of the past.

After a couple of minutes I came to a little pathway leading to a memorial set back from the road. In July 1923, at the height of the Civil War, Noel Lemass, brother of Seán Lemass, was captured by Free State forces and unofficially executed. The hatred that inspired both sides at the time was such that his family were not even given back the body; instead it was interred secretly on this spot. His mother knew he had been killed and was distraught at not being able to give her son a proper burial. Eventually, three months later, one of those involved in his death had word passed to the family where to find his body and it was finally re-buried in the family plot. The inscription on the memorial is taken from Terence McSwiney's oration over Tomás McCurtin's grave:

> He has lived a beautiful life, and has left a beautiful field, he has sacrificed the hour to give service for all time; he has entered the company of the great, and with them, he will be remembered forever.

A few minutes after leaving the Lemass memorial I was descending a narrow tarmac road into deep, picturesque Glenasmole. The valley is a carved glacial hollow in the Dublin hills following the route of the Dodder river back up to its source high on the slopes of Kippure Mountain near the Wicklow county border. The curtain of morning mist and low cloud which had filled the valley up to now had drawn back to the south and east as if sucked out by the sun, leaving a jig-saw of shadows on the bracken-covered flanks of Corrig Mountain. Acres of lazy beds patterned the slopes, indelible shapes in the earth left by the labour of those who farmed smallholdings and lived out their lives here long ago. Even the summit of Seahan, where I hoped to be later in the day, was now clearly visible. I felt mildly dismayed to see how far I would have to descend into the valley before climbing again to Seahan.

Although little evidence survives in the glen of early man's occupation of the place, the surrounding summits are all topped by sepulchral monuments dating back to the neolithic period, and Glenasmole is mentioned by name in Celtic mythology as being one of the places where the hero Finn MacCumhal hunted with his Fianna. A large erratic boulder in the valley is named Finn MacCumhal's Stone on ordnance maps, as it has been in local Fenian tales for centuries, and three of the summits to the west of the valley, Seefin, Seefingan and Ballymorefinn bear the hero's name.

The valley is also named in one of the most famous of the legends relating to Finn's son, Oisin. He had fallen in love with Niamh, the daughter of the king of Tir na nOg, the Land of Never-Ending Youth, and she took him back home with her to the mystic land across the sea. There they married and lived so happily that he did not feel the time passing; after 300 years, he felt he had only been there three. He was anxious to visit his home to see his father and friends but when Niambh tried to persuade him that by now they had all passed away, he would not believe her. Seeing she could not persuade him, she gave him a white horse with golden shoes for the journey, and warned him not to touch the soil of Erin or he would never return. On his arrival back in Erin, Oisin was horrified to find that everything had changed, and the people he met were small and puny. When he came to Glenasmole, the people told him that Finn and the Fianna had died long ago. They asked him to help them lift a large boulder that lay in the glen. Leaning forward on his steed, Oisin managed to raise the stone but suddenly the girth of his saddle broke with the strain, and he fell to the ground. Immediately, the magical horse galloped off into the west, and when Oisin got to his feet, he found his youth had deserted him; he had become an old man with a bent back and wrinkled skin. As I walked downhill into Glenasmole with ravens circling overhead, I thought that any one of the boulders scattered among the gorse bushes on either side of the road could have been the one that resulted in Oisin's downfall.

At the southern end of the valley I could see, rising above a dense grove of trees, stone chimneys and a steeply pitched roof. This was the 'big house' of the valley, Glenasmole

Lodge, built in 1792 by George Grierson, the King's printer in Ireland. He was a very rich man and entertained sumptuously and frequently, filling the valley with the sounds of music and merriment. Grierson's three daughters were great travellers and after Grierson's death, they altered the lodge, converting it into a Swiss chalet with a steep thatched roof and an external balcony of richly carved wood. They filled the house with the skins of wild beasts and antlers of great deer, mementoes of their travels, and planted many rare shrubs and rhododendrons in the grounds. They took a proprietorial interest in the peasants of the valley, and introduced woodcarving in the Swiss style as a cottage industry; I am told that specimens of the work of that period are still to be found in local houses. During the Second World War the house was shared as a shooting lodge by the Dean of Christchurch and Sir John Maffey, the British Representative in Dublin. It was extensively refurbished in 1964, incorporating interior features such as fireplaces, doors and architraves salvaged from a variety of exceptional Dublin houses that have since disappeared.

I left the unenclosed moorland behind as I reached the outskirts of the hamlet called Cunard, a place of tiny cottages and clotheslines, echoing with the barking of dogs. Between the clustered dwellings were haggards scattered with the remains of ancient agricultural equipment, red rusting mangles, parts of horse-drawn ploughs, and cast iron feed cauldrons. In one place I saw an almost intact circle of mushroom-shaped stones called staddels, which were used to keep corn stacks off the ground and out of reach of vermin in days gone by two black-and-white mongrel collies appeared menacingly from a gateway ahead of me and I prepared myself for a head-on confrontation, but as I drew nearer they hopped back behind their boundary, without letting up on their barking tirade.

At Cunard I turned south and headed down into Castlekelly, an autumn mecca years ago for my family when out foraging for the juiciest blackberries of County Dublin. It was only later that I found the size and taste of the Glenasmole berries were long renowned; Nora O'Mahony, a sister of novelist and poet Katherine Tynan, wrote in 1908 of Glenasmole: 'such blackberries! Great luscious giants of fellows, hanging heavily and in unlimited profusion on the long vine-like stems ...'

At Castlekelly bridge I crossed the Dodder river and turned westwards once again. The river was formerly a more substantial stream here than it is today, since most of the water was diverted further upstream as part of the Bohernabreena waterworks constructed in the nineteenth century.

At what is called the 'new' Castlekelly bridge I crossed another broad watercourse flowing down towards the Bohernabreena reservoirs. In the 1880s what is now the district of Rathmines was an expanding township with its own local authority, and to ensure the continuation of adequate water supplies, then running at one and a half million gallons per day, a new reservoir was constructed in this deep glacial valley. Although at a distance it looks a simple enough construction, there were a number of problems about the site which were solved with typical Victorian thoroughness and ingenuity. The main problems included how to avoid using the peat-stained Dodder for tap water and how to ensure that the large number of watermills in operation downstream on the river continued to enjoy a sufficient supply of water. The construction of two reservoirs, one above the other, was the solution devised. The upper reservoir collected the pure 'potable' waters that flowed from the ground immediately above the valley and piped them into Rathmines, while the peaty water of the upper Dodder was cleverly diverted down past the higher reservoir to the lower one, from where its release into the lower reaches of the river is controlled.

As I passed by the gate I began to ascend again and started on a long climb towards the highest point of my route to Galway, Seahan Mountain, 657m above sea-level. Turning up a narrow side road, I crossed a culvert over one of the streams feeding the reservoir below, its thundering descent almost drowning out the song of a thrush, perched nearby in an elderberry bush. The bird thrust its speckled breast out boldly, as if it knew that it had a special place here in the Glen of the Thrushes, which is the English translation of Glenasmole. St John Gogarty wrote of a thrush he came across near here:

Do you remember that thrush at Glenasmole
In the high lane on the west side when I made the engine
    stop.
When he perched across the roadway as if demanding
    toll:
So well within his rights was he, he would not even hop?

Continuing steeply up the hill I passed through a cluster of slated cottages, some of them well-built with cut-stone quoins, all with tiny windows suggesting their age and the harshness of the winter weather here. The tarmac soon ran out, and I carried on along a track that ran through a farmyard. I quickened my step gingerly when another dog began a tirade of barking, this one unseen, concealed in a kennel

made from a disused oil tank which amplified the sound and gave it a strange, hollow effect. Finally reaching open mountainside again, I steadily ascended an old bog road that sliced up along the north eastern slopes of Seahan. J.B. Malone tells of an old man he talked to here in the townsland of Allagour, who told him that the road had been used 'by thousands of men, long ago', and I recall reading somewhere of a sugges-

45

tion that Richard de Clare, or Strongbow, had brought his army this way towards the end of his march from Waterford to the Danish city of Dublin in 1170 AD. If this is true, I was following a very ancient route. The surface was soft grass and clover, grazed by sheep to a smooth carpet texture, and it made for a comfortable climb. At almost every step the views broadened richly behind. The reservoir below was like a dark mirror reflecting the other side of the valley; off to the north the suburbs of Dublin reached out westwards into the plains of Kildare. Beyond Montpelier Hill I could see the papal cross standing out white against the green of the Phoenix Park.

As the altitude increased the number of grazing sheep decreased until my only companions were two soaring ravens, honking continually to one another as they gloried in the updraughts. I was slowing down a little now as the surface of the bog road gradually deteriorated. At a little waterfall beside the road, I cupped my hands and drank a half-dozen palmfuls of deliciously cold and refreshing water. An ominous black cloud was heading my way from the north with a threat of rain; I was planning to have my lunch on the summit, and I hoped it would keep off at least until I was comfortably finished. I debated with myself as to whether I should start getting into my rain gear or not, but as there was no sign yet of telltale, dark washes in the sky below the cloud I decided to keep going.

I left the bog road when I sensed its highest point had been reached, and crossed open moorland in a westerly direction towards where I expected to find the summit of Seahan. Soon I was relieved to see a pole on the horizon to the south that marked the otherwise featureless summit of neighbouring Corrig Mountain, 76 feet lower than Seahan, and knew that Seahan was near; just before 1pm, and right on time for lunch, I reached its windy summit.

Seahan seems to be always raked by strong winds that whistle around its cairn of stones; one walker, describing the place in 1912, said, 'The wind howled on the summit. It was cold. It was damp. Grey mist had buried the valleys, the wind was keening for the dead.' It was hard to believe that one December day, with some walking companions, I basked in my shirtsleeves in warm sun here, and not a breath of air stirred. Below us, a fog enveloped the land, and only the surrounding mountain peaks protruded from it, like islands in a brilliant white sea. But for that one time, it has always seemed to be quite miserable.

To the north and west were the foothills of the Dublin mountains, and beyond them, Kildare stretched westwards. I could trace most of the route that lay before me for the rest of the day, over Tallaght Hill and Saggart Hill to that long esker-like ridge that reaches south towards Blessington. To the south and east were bare, rounded mountains, some nippled with burial cairns like the one that crowns Seahan. Seahan's 25m diameter cairn of stones, surmounted by an ordnance trig point, is the most obvious, but certainly not the only, monument to be built on its summit by prehistoric man. To its north east, much less discernable, is a disturbed Bronze-Age burial mound, probably built 1,500 years after the larger neolithic cairn, and there are at least two more, smaller, cist-type burial places nearby. At one time I had, in my ignorance, assumed that the large cairns were the later monuments, the product of a more advanced race, while the modest stone-lined cists were the work of a 'lesser', more primitive, Stone-Age people. It was an eye-opener to later discover that while the smaller 'cist' type burials, stone-lined

pits, were actually Bronze Age, the most elaborate of our prehistoric burial or ceremonial monuments belong to the late
Stone Age, an indication of the state of the cultural development of those early peoples. Newgrange, Knowth and
Dowth, those prodigious passage tombs overlooking the
river Boyne, all represent the age of stone, and give some
insight into the sophistication of a society that the old stereo-
type of animal skin garments, wooden clubs and ape-like
appearance got so wrong. The name Seahan comes from the
Gaelic for seat; old maps of the area show the name as
'Seacenisknabantre' which could be loosely translated as 'the
seat of the widow's son'. The reason for this name, probably
associated with the old traditions relating to the burial
mound, is lost in the past.

Stone cairns covering passages and burial chambers similar to the larger one on Seahan are to be found on a considerable number of summits in these mountains; on nearby
Seefin the stone lintelled entrance to a passage is exposed,
and one can squeeze through to reach the chamber, which is
now open to the sky. I believe communities of neolithic people lived on these mountain tops, their dwellings gathered
around their burial monuments like a village around a
church. More recent examples of this form are common
throughout hilly areas all over southern Europe, where cli-
matic conditions are probably similar to what prevailed in
Ireland nearly five millennia ago. On the saddle between
nearby Seefin and Seefingan, pollen extracted from cores of
the soil at the base of the peat some years ago showed a
decline in elms and pines was followed by the appearance of
plantain, evidence that indicates this high land was cleared
and farmed in neolithic times before the bog began to develop. The climate then was milder, and the thin soil of the

mountains would have encouraged only sparse forest, so the trees would have been easier to clear to create pastures compared to the lowlands, which would have been covered with a thick impenetrable wildwood. Only a reliable supply of water would have been needed to make settlements possible on these summits. I have never been able to find one on Seahan, but St John Joyce, writing nearly 100 years ago in *The Neighbourhood of Dublin*, mentions finding a spring here, 'the source of a small stream that runs down the western slope of the mountain'.

I sat on the capstone of the Bronze-Age construction and ate my lunch, keeping a close eye on the rain clouds which seemed to be multiplying as they rolled along from the north. As I savoured my coffee I could feel the cold begin to seep into my limbs, so I did not delay, packed up again and set off downhill.

Dropping down a series of fire breaks between trees, I followed a vague path northwards to reach a forestry road. As I emerged from the trees and stepped down onto the road there was a car parked in against the earth bank. I saw, with a mild shock, that there was a naked couple in the back seat engaged in some sort of sexual contortions, arms and legs everywhere. Their activities were so busy and vigorous that they either did not see me or took no notice of me passing.

The track led me to the public road west of Ballymorefin Hill. A mile to the south along this road there is a cottage which is said to be, at 430m above sea level, the highest occupied dwelling in Ireland.

Seahan receded behind and finally disappeared from view as I entered Ballinascorney Wood and descended into the valley of the Brittas River. Splintered tree stumps and heaps of brush lined the forestry road. Killinarden Hill had looked low and easy from the summit of Seahan, but now, from the lowest point of the valley, it loomed ahead formidably.

Soon the road became a green mossy-covered track that had once been the demesne avenue of Ballinascorney House, and as the conifers all round gave way to much older, mixed deciduous trees, the sad, burnt-out ruins of the house came into view. It was formerly called Dillon Lodge after the Dillons of Belgard who built it as a shooting-box. The Bagenal family were living in it in 1803 when it was captured by Robert Emmet and some of his men escaping from the failed rising in Dublin. When Emmet returned to the out-skirts of Dublin he was captured and died on the gallows not long after at the age of 25. A later owner of the house was Major Knox, founder and first proprietor of *The Irish Times*.

Of the pleasure gardens that were formerly attached to the house little remained other than a few stately copper beeches and leylandias and what was left of an ornamental pond. The pond, through which the Brittas River flowed, had a rhododendron-covered island, but was almost solid with weed. Further along, the avenue crossed the river by way of a once ornate bridge, and ascended to pass between rusting cast-iron gate-posts to reach the public road. A large sign at the entrance gate said, 'Lands strictly preserved; Trespassers prosecuted'.

A short distance on the main road brought me to a nar-row laneway leading steeply up Killinarden Hill, and I paused halfway to take a breath and look back. Seahan was almost in darkness under a black cloud, while out to the east, the Hill of Howth basked in brilliant sunshine on an azure Dublin Bay, the Bailey lighthouse glittering at the end of the head. At this stage I was walking under a low corridor of cloud, while to either side, west and east, the sun shone brightly from a blue sky; it was like looking out from under a great roof. Although a threatening sky had promised rain for the previous couple of hours, none had come, and I wondered how much longer I would escape a downpour.

As I passed a cottage I looked for a sign of life, but was disappointed. Passing this way on a previous occasion I had met a tiny woman dressed in track-suit bottoms, a thick cardigan and a woolly hat, sweeping at the cottage gateway here. She was of indeterminate age, anywhere between 40 and 70, with a fresh complexion and twinkling eyes.

'Ooooh, you gave me a fright, did you come out from the fields?' she had asked.

I told her I had come up the road and she laughed;

'You're after coming up the road, I never seen you, 'she said still laughing. 'Are you shootin' or what?'

I explained I was walking to Kilteel, and she said I was not going the right way. I explained that I did not want to walk on the road, preferring to go cross-country.

'Isn't it well for you,' she joked, 'an' me hard at work sweepin'. Are you from Kilteel?'

I explained that I lived near Rathfarnham, to which she quickly replied, 'This place was in the parish of Rathfar'm one time. My husband, lord have mercy on him, made his Confirmation in Rathfar'm. He was christened in Bohernabreena, but had to go to Rathfar'm for Confirmation.'

We chatted on as she skilfully but gently interrogated me and found out I was from Waterford originally.

'I was there recently, it was spilling rain, no wonder they call it "Water' ford!" she laughed.

I asked her if I was in Malachi Horan country, referring to a Killinarden man whose stories of the area in the nineteenth century had been published in the 1940s.

'Ah, right,' she said. 'Listen, do you believe all he said, do you? My husband was born and reared, and his mother was too, up there, and he said it was all a pack o' lies! Somethin' just to get the book out. Sure I could tell a pack o' lies too for money,' she laughed.

I asked about the ice-houses that there used to be on the hillside here before refrigeration was invented.

'My husband's grandfather kept the ice in one up there, a hole in the ground. The field is still called the "ice-house field", and they used draw it to Dublin in a horse and cart. The family house is just a heap of stones up at the top of the road now; my husband's mother, she was 88 whan she died, and she's 23 years dead, was born and reared there. They gave a lend of the house to another family. There were five girls and three boys reared in it; the boys went to America, because of the father.'

Although we were alone on the hillside she lowered her voice to say, 'and the girls stood, and they used to take in washing from down in the city, and bring it up here to wash it and get a bit of a livin'. Sure the girls had to go after the plough because there were no boys left. They weren't allowed out late at night, and they used to get out through the window to go dancing! It wasn't dances in a dance hall, but house dances, the "Breedo" we used call it. You have a dance in your house one night, and we would have it here another night. God be with the days we used to go dancing!'

She talked on happily with lots of laughter, about her own childhood home in the Slade of Saggart, the steam tram to Blessington, the old coach road, and a place called Judy's Pinch, near where I would pass later in the day. This name intrigued me and I asked her what the story was behind it.

'Well I used often hear them sayin' this fella and girl were going with one another, you see, and they were having a bit of love, and he gave her a pinch, and she died from it. And her name was Judy.'

She wished me luck and told me she had enjoyed our 'little chat'. I was looking forward to meeting her again this time but it was not to be.

Near the top of the road I entered the coniferous forest that covers the top of Killinarden hill, and turned towards the west again. Also known as Knockanavea, Killinarden is little known even amongst south County Dubliners, but this northern outlier of the Dublin Mountains has a special character. The stories told by the old lady I had met, about the people who had lived here, are confirmed in the writings of the poet Nora O'Mahony, who used to visit the area at the turn of the nineteenth and twentieth centuries. At the time it was a popular place of resort for Victorian fern-collectors and blackberry pickers who were welcomed by the kindly and hospitable farmfolk. The hill was dotted with prosperous farmhouses and cottages, which would ring at evening time with song and fiddle and flute music.

Half-a-mile away over the hill, near the summit, Malachi Horan, whom I had discussed with the old lady, lived for much of his life. He had reached the age of 96 in 1943 when his reminiscences were written down by Dr George Little and published in *Malachi Horan Remembers*. Most of the work is written in parenthesis, a verbatim record of the old sage's words, the setting down of which was an achievement in the days before tape recorders were common.

After a long stretch in the trees I came out of the forest on the western side of Killinarden, and straight ahead I could see my next goal, the top of wooded Saggart Hill, which I could see to the north-west. I skirted along the forest edge passing one of the many prehistoric burial mounds that one can find on Killinarden, and crossed a field to reach a narrow road.

The land off to the south towards Blessington is part of a large farm, where many fields have been made into one or two, creating a great expanse of lush pastureland fringed with trees like a Rembrandtian landscape. Years ago, just after the fields had been joined, I remember searching in one of them for a ringfort which was clearly shown on the ordnance map. After much walking through the harrowed fields my companion pointed out an area where the soil was a slightly different colour; the patch turned out to be of a circular shape, and about the right dimension. The ringfort we were looking for had, it seemed, not long before been ploughed in, as is a common fate of ringforts, the remains of Irish farmsteads of the early Christian period. There are still more than 20,000 surviving in our countryside, making them our most numerous archaeological monument, but it is clear that far more have been destroyed during the past century in agricultural improvements. In their original form they would have been surrounded by high banks of earth covered with a thick blackthorn hedge, protecting the farmstead dwellings and outhouses inside. They had gone out of use by 1,000 AD but unless destroyed, their earthen rings will decorate our landscape for many centuries to come.

I had now entered the townsland of Crooksling, a place that has had the benefit of considerable scholarly attention in relation to its history, placenames and folklore. In the 1940s Liam Ua Broin set about collecting, noting and suggesting origins of its placenames, which he published in the *Journal of the Royal Irish Academy*. I had brought a copy with me, and it told me that the almost circular field to my right was

named Coolcott, which Ua Broin suggested might be a cor-
ruption of the Gaelic *cúl na cruite* (back of the hump-like
hill), or *cúil na cruite,* (corner of the hump-like hill). He also
mentioned a nearby field which was called 'Plawsane
Gurtawn', and suggested that the name was probably derived
from the Gaelic *Plásán na ngart-éan* (the level or smooth
place of the corncrakes) or alternatively *Plásán a' Ghortáin*
(the place of the stingy person). What interesting clues about
the past can come from explanations of placenames.

I got a final glimpse of the south-western suburbs of
Dublin before I entered the forestry on Saggart Hill and made
my way westwards in search of a route that would bring me
down to the main Blessington road. After a while I could
hear the traffic on the road below me, so I turned off the
forestry track and headed down, sliding over a deep bed of
leaves, through the trees in the direction of the sound. I had
come this way before but was still surprised at how steep it
was. At the bottom, the bonnet of a car lying with assorted
trays in the bracken suggested that the place is frequently
used, as a kind of toboggan run.

The Blessington Road was an aural and nasal shock, with
heavy traffic thundering along both ways at speed, leaving
invisible clouds of diesel fumes, and an unavoidable stench. I
dodged gingerly along the road, skipping across and down a
steep narrow side road, Judy's Pinch, a name which I was surprised to find was mentioned in the ua Broin paper I was carrying. He suggested that the Judy was Judith Askins, who
had a cottage at the roadside here in 1844, the remains of
which have only recently disappeared.

As soon as I could I climbed a roadside hedge and
descended across a field into the wooded valley of the River
Camac, leaving behind the noise of traffic and replacing it

with the restful sibilance of running water. I followed a track that meandered south with the riverbank through an idyllic glen, watching out for a way across to the far bank. There were a number of fallen trees spanning the water but none looked safe enough to trust. Soon, however, I came level with a tiny island that was linked to each bank by a shallow ford with stepping stones, and here I crossed without getting my feet wet. On the far side I climbed a steep bank, its surface laced with the roots of the beech trees above, looking like half-submerged, mossy serpents.

Crossing a road, I entered another forest and climbed steadily through the trees and out into the open on Coolmine Hill. The views east and south now in the sinking sun were extensive and very fine. Seahan was still haunting my steps, and would be for many a mile more, but now, with some relief, I could look back at Saggart Hill and Killinarden beyond; only three more hills left! I followed a riding club's trekking trail west to reach a road, and after a short distance entered Slievethoul Wood, which covers a hill called Knockananiller, from the Gaelic *Cnoc an Iolar,* meaning the rock of the eagle. The name must hark back a long way, because it is surely two centuries since eagles were seen here.

I sought the summit of the hill by following each forestry road that seemed to climb, eventually arrived into a broad area of cleared forest with a marvellous vista to the west, where I got my first view of the part of Kildare that I would cross on the next stage of my walk, and the Central Plain beyond. To the north Slieve Gullion in County Armagh and the soft serrations of the Mourne Mountains could just be distinguished in the evening sun.

Knockananiller is one of four hill summits over 300m high within half a mile of one another, topped with important prehistoric monuments. The hills and countryside around must have been heavily populated for a long period at least the 3,000 years from the Neolithic right through to the Iron Age, because evidence of their passing, in the form of the remains of eleven known ceremonial sites of various periods, survive, scattered over the four hill-tops. My research had told me that the great cairn here on Knockananiller, concealing a passage and chamber constructed from granitic monoliths, was probably one of the oldest of the monuments, dating from about 3,000 BC. I had thought that the thick forestry would prevent me from finding it but I was pleasantly surprised to come upon, in the midst of the harvested forestry, an extensive bracken-covered mound near the highest point of the hill. I made my way over to it across a tangle of lopped branches and climbed to it's top. The mound, about 50m in diameter, had unfortunately become part of the local riding clubs hacking route. A trench-like track was cut through the thin soil covering, exposing and disturbing the stone cairn underneath. A short distance to the north of the cairn I found the remains of a small passage grave. Of the third monument that is said to be on this hill, a raised platform probably built in the Iron-Age as part of a ceremonial site, I could find no trace.

On the next summit to the south, in the midst of gantries, aerials and radar-like communications dishes, camouflaged by a covering of heather and fraughans, I found another low-lying stone-kerbed mound thousands of years old, it's presence for me more powerful than all the surrounding high-tech hardware.

At the western end of Slievethoul Wood I emerged onto the public road near two burnt-out cars. Ahead lay green and rounded Cromwellstown Hill topped with another communications mast, and beyond it Cupidstown Hill, at 378m, the highest point in County Kildare. To the east and south the rolling Dublin Mountains became the Wicklow Mountains, summit after summit as far as the eye could see. Seahan seemed so far away, beyond Seefin and Seefingan, and, but for my aching muscles, it was hard to believe that I had been there just a few hours earlier.

After a few minutes I crossed out of County Dublin into County Kildare; to the west and south now the Central Plain extended to the horizon with few interruptions. On a hill about 3km to the south west I could see a cluster of white painted buildings; my destination for the day, the village of Kilteel.

Due to its proximity to Dublin, Kildare's population has been increasing over the past decades. Early in the 1800s the county had a population of 108,000, and this number was hardly exceeded until the 1970s, when Dublin began to spread out; today Kildare is home to upwards of 145,000 people, mostly concentrated in the prosperous north-east region. My route would take me along a corridor through the north of the county, south of the booming town of Leixlip, where vast manufacturing complexes are located, and north of Newbridge, finally through one of the poorest parts of the county, the eastern reaches of the Bog of Allen.

I had to stand right into the hedge as a heavy lorry, drawing a cloud of dust, bore down on me, coming from a near-by quarry where Cromwellstown Hill is used in the erection of man-made hills of office blocks and apartments. The little country road I was following could not cope with the traffic and was in a state of collapse, its hedges of hawthorn and gorse coated with a fine white dusting. Near the entrance to the quarry there is a roadside memorial commemorating

Michael Sullivan. A man nearby was sweeping up the dust deposited by the lorries outside his house and I asked him what he knew about it.

'No, no, no, it was a long time ago,' he replied. 'I suppose he was killed there, I've only been here this twenty year'.

I asked him if I could get up onto Cromwellstown Hill, and he told me that I could not cross the quarry, and it was dangerous crossing the fields.

'There's fences and wan thing an' another, then you've cattle and you've a bull runnin' with them, and you're likely to get attacked. You have to be very very careful, they'd kill you in a second! There was a fellow killed a few years ago down my country, of a Saharday mornin'. There was this man come with a heifer, he had the bull up at the back of the house. He said hold on now and I'll be back, I'll go up and bring him down'

He paused for effect, and in an almost inaudible voice he continued, 'He never came back, that was the end of him, he was down and they couldn't save him, the poor childer and the wife, she collapsed. The bull went beserk, sure he'd go through that,' he indicated the sturdy wooden fence in front of his house.

'I'd be terrified myself of one, he'd take the nose offa him.'

Then he abruptly changed the subject and asked,

'Are ye walking then?'

I told him I was heading for Kilteel, and as he was clearly recommending against going over the fields, I'd go by the road after all. He wished me well and went back to his sweeping, a job which, with the constant to-ing and fro-ing of lorries, must be a bit like painting the Golden Gate bridge.

I was tired and relieved that I would not to have to climb

another hill. As I set off downhill I could see, away in the distance, lines of vehicles moving along the Naas Road. Slightly to the north, the stump of a windmill identified Windmill Hill for me, and then I was able to recognise beyond it Athgoe Hill, its earthen-banked prehistoric platform visible on its summit, and behind it, Lyons Hill, with its mohican fringe of trees.

For every robust and austere old cottage and tin-roofed shed I passed there were two new bungalows, bigger, brash and glossy. At last I crossed a little bridge and started the last short ascent of the day up into Kilteel. I counted the seventh runaway hub-cap of the evening since I had left the wood on Slievethoul, high up in a tree, glinting silvery like a Christmas decoration as I entered the village and made straight for the pub for a much-needed sit down and a pint.

From Kilteel to Johnstown,
County Kildare

At 700 feet above sea level Kilteel is the highest village in County Kildare. It is a place of tiny public gardens, well-kept bungalows and a neat and simple slated church with a belfry reminiscent of pre-penal examples. The interior is narrow and long with an intimate scale, under a neatly-detailed timber roof structure. I find that most Roman Catholic churches do not display information about their history, date of erection, or even the saint to whom the church is dedicated. It is a pity; one would think that it would be a useful reminder for parishioners of the parish's history and traditions, apart altogether from satisfying the curiosity of visitors. Kilteel church looked like it dated from the early to mid-twentieth century, and a brass plate in the porch dated July 1934 commemorating Mr and Mrs James McGuinness 'who erected the walls of this church' confirmed this.

The Kilteel Inn occupies a prominent place in the village centre, next to the original primary school, which a stone tablet claims was established in 1845. Most of the modern village is secluded to the west of the main street, but for signs of Kilteel's ancient past you must look to the east and south

across the fields. Little remains of the early Christian monastery which is said to have been established here, but opposite the pub, close to the road, a few fragments of medieval carved stonework lie forlornly in a barbed wire enclosure. Beyond, down in a shallow marshy valley, a solitary heap of masonry stands in a field; the other extremity of the building complex to which this belonged, two massive pieces of masonry, one of them part of an arch, is 100m to the south. This is all that remains of a great outpost of the Dublin Pale, a preceptory of the Knights Hospitallers founded in AD 1212 by the Norman knight Maurice Fitzgerald. Looking at the scale of these remains one wonders at the size the original preceptory must have been, and at the ferocity of the religious wars that led to its utter destruction.

Down a narrow road to the east you can find a gem of medieval church architecture – in ruin of course, but with sufficient surviving to give a good impression of what it was like when complete. The chancel arch is decorated with some of the most delicate twelfth-century stone carving you will find in Ireland, depicting biblical subjects like Adam and Eve, David with the head of Goliath, as well as a wonderful scene of two wrestlers in a close clinch with the braids of their long hair interwoven. East of the church are earthworks that have been identified as the remains of the thirteenth-century Pale ditch, associated with the nearby preceptory.

It was late in the morning when I left Kilteel. I had resolved to make it an easy day; my goal was Johnstown, only about 10km away, all on tarmac unfortunately, but by way of quiet side roads and laneways.

As I left the village I passed another remnant of Kilteel's past, a tall sixteenth-century tower-house with an arched gateway. Opposite it were a row of bungalows with names like Glenshiel, Timber Vale, Naombh Antoin and Castle Cove, their styles as diverse as their names. Bungalows continued along the roadside; after a mile I had passed just one traditional farm cottage. AI tried to conjure up some positive aspects of the ribbon development of detached homes that characterises Ireland's countryside today without success. In social terms and energy conservation terms this solution to housing is ludicrous; in architectural terms it results in a

Disneyland countryside, and the thousands of septic tanks pollute the land and the ground water. Village or hamlet gatherings of dwellings are better, serving to create self-sufficient and interactive communities, and making the provision and maintenance of all the services needed – garbage collection, sewerage, electrical and telecommunications, transport and fuel deliveries – more economic in every way. Ribbon development creates unconnected units, independent in the worst of ways, where people do not get the opportunity to interact with their neighbours. In visual terms, clusters of buildings in the landscape are easier to handle, leaving the rest of the countryside free and clear for agricultural or amenity development. Unfortunately, what has happened is almost impossible to reverse, fraught as it is by the multiplication and dispersal of land ownership.

I soon saw a thickly wooded area ahead, from the centre of which a church tower was silhouetted against the sky, indicating the next village on my route, Rathmore, was near. As I came closer I could see that the trees consisted of beeches and ash interspersed with Scots pines and wellingtonias, evidence of the fashion of planting demesnes of exotic trees that began in the eighteenth century and lasted until into the twentieth, but is rarely initiated today. I crossed over a fast-flowing river and walked up into Rathmore between two high walls. The village consists of a neat row of two-storey cottages, a fine and extensive glebe house built in the 1820s, and a Church of Ireland church built in the late eighteenth century; the most significant feature of the place, however, is the grassy mound beside the church, the 'big rath', which gives the place its name. Local histories suggest that the Normans converted the original Gaelic ceremonial rath into a typical motte and bailey, constructing a timber castle on top of the mound. Whatever its history, it is impressive and has suffered little from the erosion that other examples have borne in places of larger population. The mound must be 15m over the level of the adjacent road, and the earthen embankment surrounding it is still 6m high. I climbed a neat stone stile and clambered over an outer embankment before I could ascend steeply onto the mound. It was easy to see that the addition of a timber palisade on the earthen mound would have created a virtually impregnable fort. The only damage the monument has suffered during all the years since its construction appears to be the removal, some time in the recent past, of the northern part of the outer rampart.

I sat in the grass on top of the motte, where the timber palisaded fort would have stood, and took off my boots and socks, luxuriating in the feel of the cool grass. The socks were a little too thick for my boots, and were giving me a certain amount of discomfort. I was unusually well equipped, however, and was able to change into a spare pair which were lighter before sitting back, taking a few sips from my water bottle, and taking in the view from my vantage point. The flat and fertile lands of Kildare stretched northwards, and to the north west I could see, reflecting the morning sun, a great slab of a building that could only be Castletown, the great Georgian mansion built by Speaker Conolly in the early eighteenth century. Of my route ahead, Forenaghts Hill blocked my view of Johnstown. I lay in the sun awhile, enjoying the soft mattress of grass and listening to a thrush singing in a nearby tree, before reluctantly donning my boots and scrambling down to the road again.

I set off heading westwards once more with the sun on my shoulder rather than in my eyes as it had been for the previous hour. The road was wider and better paved than from

Kilteel, and the cars were moving faster. The surrounding countryside was changing as I headed west; I was now passing through a landscape of large farms with vast, manicured fields bordered by well-trimmed hedges and carefully placed beeches and Scots pines. The serenading of robins backed by the sibilance of a stream flowing unseen behind the roadside hedge accompanied me as I strode along, warmed by the sun and feeling great. Even the roaring of bulldozers on the top of nearby Arthurstown 'landfill' and the increasing number of four-wheel-drive vehicles which roared past me failed to dampen my spirits.

It was almost one o'clock when I began feeling that I was finally in the country, as opposed to the suburbs of Dublin. After a surge that lasted a few minutes, the constant traffic on the road reduced to almost nothing, and it was clear that it was because everyone had gone home to their dinner, a tradition that has been lost in the urban and suburban areas of Ireland.

On Forenaghts Hill I had what I thought was my last glimpse of the mountains, reduced to grey-blue hills now, and from such an unfamiliar angle I could only guess that the summits I was saying farewell to were Sorrel Hill and Mullacleevaun. I descended a hill along the demesne wall of Furness Hall which I was to follow for nearly 2km, and turned down a narrow road between the Forenaghts and Furness demesnes. A little further on I came to the entrance gates of Forenaghts House; the mansion was visible through the trees, sited at the end of an elegantly curved avenue. It was built in the middle of the eighteenth century, and has been much altered and extended since into a large stud farm. A very large house, it was the home of the Anglo-Irish Wolfe family from the middle of the eighteenth century until 1980 and had many distinguished members: General James Wolfe fought at the battles of Detingen, Culloden and Laffeldt, and commanded the British forces in the taking of Quebec in 1759; The Rev Charles Wolfe was referred to as 'the little-known Irish poet' in Samuel Beckett's *Happy Days*, being best-known for his elegiac poem of the Peninsular Wars *The Burial of Sir John Moore*. The occupier of Forenaghts at time of the 1798 rebellion, Colonel John Wolfe, led the Kildare Militia against the rebels at Naas. In a strange quirk of fate, Theobald Wolfe Tone, revolutionary, founder of Irish Republicanism and one of the instigators of the 1798 rebellion, was named after Theobald Wolfe, another member of the family who owned the Blackhall estate near Clane, on which Tone's father was employed as the coachmaker.

On the opposite side of the road I passed an elegant building with friezes and a cylindrical granite chimney, the gate-lodge of Furness Hall. The gateway is modest, of rusticated granite piers each displaying a tiny sandstone flower motif. The house itself came into view a little further on; a very fine three-storey, three-bay house of the 1740s with a doorcase flanked by twin Doric columns. It is attributed to the architect Francis Bindon and is a great example of the gutsy, gritty architecture of the early Georgian period, before everything became subdued, refined and spare. Just inside the demesne wall, on an axis with the front of the house, is a tall column topped by the figure of Mercury. It was originally in the grounds of Dangan Castle in County Meath, the boyhood home of the Duke of Wellington, and was re-erected here in 1962 as a twenty-first birthday gift to the last owner, Mr David Synott, who sold the estate in 1987. Today the future of the house seems secure.

At a fork in the road I carried on straight, a little unsure that I was going the right way. I spotted a man coming towards me on a bicycle, the handlebars hung down with bulging plastic bags. Before he reached me, however, he dismounted and disappeared from view behind a hedge. Thinking he was going into a cottage, I hurried along to reach the gateway, only to find him looking out over a field, with his back to me.

'Excuse me,' I said, 'can you tell me if I am on the right road for Johnstown?'

He fumbled with his trousers and turning, said 'I was havin' a wee-wee, sorry.'

A little embarrassed at disturbing him, I repeated my question. He did not seem to be bothered.

'You could have turned off up there, off to your right but you can go this way too.'

'Which is the shorter?' I asked.

'When you go that way it's a nice scenic walk, you take the first turn left.'

He was a small man of indeterminate age, wearing a black woollen hat, an old leather jacket, and threadbare trousers tucked into his socks. As he talked he reached into one of the bags hanging on the bike and, taking out a handful of bread, began to throw pieces to a robin that had appeared from nowhere, now trilling on a nearby branch.

I asked him who owned Forenaghts House now.

His demeanour changed a little, and he muttered, 'I don't know who's there now. This used to belong to Mrs Wolfe,' he indicated to the Forenaghts demesne. 'She wouldn't sell an inch of land in it either, and you could come through on your bike. There was an old gate there and you could come out at that corner. But all these new people coming in, they all build their "Gone with the Wind" gates, and block your passage. You'd wonder, you know. History repeating itself.'

He continued to throw bread after the departing robin. 'They were very scarce for a while,' he said, referring to robins. 'I've been living up here for twenty years, and I have a river in the back garden where we used to see dippers and a big crane going after the fingerlings.' He pronounced it 'crayen' and I found he was a Dublin man, but one who had travelled all over.

A large four-wheel drive jeep came speeding down the narrow road and we had to move into the gateway to make room for its passage.

'What do they need those big cars for?' he asked. 'I was in Australia for ten years and they needed big cars there. I was in Chicago for fourteen months in the 1960s and used to walk along the shores of Lake Michigan at night time. It's supposed to be the land of gangsters. I lived near Clarke Street where the Valentine's Day Massacre happened, but nobody ever bothered me. I'll tell you though, I found out, and it wasn't at school, that Lake Michigan is the exact size of Ireland, 150 miles across and 300 miles long. So what do they need all these cars for? You can go around this country in a day.'

He was really warming up now, and was clearly delighted he had a sympathetic ear.

'It's all show, and they're not paid for – the banks own them all! There's going to be pay-back time one of these days, and they'll be more ruthless here than anywhere else. They're embezzling money the whole feffing lot of them – politicians, the whole shagging lot, putting the poverty and deprivation in little pigeon boxes, and you can't escape unless you emigrate. I went to Australia in 1959, after working across the water, on the ten-pound passage. That woke me up. They had the minimum wage there, equal pay for women, giving them

69

a bit of dignity, and there was full employment at the time. There was discrimination against Catholics from the time of the founding fathers, but Australia is such a big country, you could put 1,000 miles between you and the next place if you wanted. By the time I went there more than 300,000 men and woman had left Ireland in eight years. Then Lemass brought a miracle in the 1960s with the low-tech economy. He was a brilliant man.'

Although I was enjoying the breathless and wonderful tirade, I was beginning to feel the pangs of hunger for lunch, which I had hoped to have at Johnstown, if I got there in time.

'And so was De Valera. He was much maligned. He got a lot of the slums out of it, as we were only a young country, and they left nothing here, that shower across the water when they left. I was born up around Grangegorman, and you could walk out your door into green fields, yet the slums in Dublin were relentless. I lived near Queen Street. There were ten families living in every house, with one toilet down the bottom and a tap. That's what the British left. Now I know they didn't give their own working classes much either, they had the whole fuckin' empire, and they're payin' for it now, I think.'

He was astonishing. His vocabulary was as rich as his bitterness was extreme.

I tried gently to cut across him, saying, 'I'll have to be on my way. I'm starving and I'm hoping to get something to eat in Johnstown.'

'Here, have one of these,' he said, taking a sweet out of his pocket. 'You shouldn't let your blood levels go down, I have a load of these'.

I accepted the sweet and unwrapping the cellophane, popped it into my mouth. I then apologised that I had to go, and thanked him for the sweet, which he assured me was pure glucose.

'Nice to see a hiker,' he called after me. 'I'm out here twenty years now, I'm a renegade, a Kildare man now. Good luck!'

I waved and marched on at a quick pace, not daring to look back for fear he might start again. After 100 yards I took a peek and saw he had remounted his bike and was slowly following, looking into the hedges, presumably for hungry birds.

I turned up the tree-lined road as he had directed me. There was a wonderful view into the parkland of the Furness demesne, where a solitary, mature lime tree stood, the bush of twigs that normally grows around the base neatly clipped by grazing sheep five feet from the ground. On the other side there was a fine vista down to Naas framed by a beech woodland. Soon I came to the outskirts of Johnstown, where extensive site works were in progress, presumably for housing, as this little village is a new suburb of Dublin.

Johnstown has for many centuries straddled the main route to the south, and grew up around an ancient church and inn. Today it is a little backwater, by-passed by Ireland's first dual carriageway, with only the roar of the constant stream of high-speed traffic going north and south to contend with. The oldest building, or remains of a building, is the 'picturesque' ruin of the pre-penal church of St John the Baptist, in which can be found a fifteenth-century graveslab decorated with the arms of the Flatebury family, who owned much of the land hereabouts from the thirteenth until the eighteenth century, and the arms of the Cromwellian Wogans, with whom the Flateburys intermarried. I was surprised to find there also a celtic cross commemorating Richard, the 6th Earl of Mayo, assassinated in 1872 while Governor-General of India.

Johnstown was not a typical Irish village, but from the

quality of the houses it obviously had been a prosperous place years ago, with inhabitants of some standing. What I liked was how the older houses and cottages have survived with dignity to the end of the twentieth century, all carefully assimilating modern components and materials without compromising their style and authenticity. I would guess this was not the result of the efforts of any inspired Planning Officer, but the combined sensitivity and good taste of the inhabitants. It is so easy to destroy all that is good in a fine old house by insulting it with ill-designed plastic windows and doors, aluminium gutters, and modern renderings, and it is to be hoped that, when the remaining houses in the main village come to be renovated, that the trend so well followed to date will be continued.

The Johnstown Inn has been renovated many times; today it sports the Shiraz Bar, with modern furniture, a surprise in such a rural setting, but making a statement on the cosmopolitan sophistication of the farming folk in County Kildare. Although it had been a relatively short walk that morning, I had built up a great appetite, and I was glad to reach the Inn. I thought lunches would be long over, but a friendly woman behind the bar assured me there was plenty left, and in no time I was sitting down to a lunch of delicious mushroom soup, followed by a beef pie.

From Johnstown to Robertstown, County Kildare

L eaving Johnstown the following morning, I crossed the Dublin to Naas dual carriageway, thick with traffic, and followed a narrow mucky road westwards. I had left the hills behind me now, and would be on the flat for at least the next 100km, following the Grand Canal route across the midlands. My destination for this, my fourth day out, was the canal harbour village of Robertstown.

The road climbed gently onto a gravel ridge from where I could see the three north Kildare hills, Allen, Grange and Dunmurray to the south west, and a scattering of white-painted suburban dwellings on the outskirts of Naas to the south. To my surprise the rounded shape of Seahan, which I had crossed two days before and which I thought I had seen the last of, was in view again, much reduced back on the eastern horizon.

The road was not great for walking and had little of interest to brighten the journey; I kept thinking how good it would be to be able to walk through the nearby rolling parkland of the Kerdifftown Estate which would deliver me almost all the way to Sallins off road. As I passed a golf course I caught a glimpse over the greens of the grey pile of Kerdiffstown House, an eighteenth-century house that has been renovated when it became a convent in the mid-twentieth century. A branch of the Aylmer family, who were shareholders in the Grand Canal, had lived here up to 1938. The house now belongs to St Vincent de Paul, and Roadstone PLC own much of the old demesne from which they extract gravel. Beyond to the north is the demesne of Palmerstown House, which belongs to entrepreneur Jim Mansfield. He made his first fortune in a most unusual but typical entrepreneurial fashion. After the defeat of the Argentinians in the Falklands War in the 1980s, the British government sold by auction an amount of civil engineering equipment and vehicles which had been used to back up the invasion and construct other infrastructure. Jim Mansfield saw the possibilities, bought the lot for a song, and did extraordinarily well when he re-sold it in Liverpool.

I rounded a corner and found the road full of scrawny white turkeys, gobbling away happily at their escape, however temporary, from a nearby farm. As I paused to take in the chaotic scene, a man and a woman came running from a nearby bungalow and began to shepherd the excited flock back through a gate to their pen and eventually, I suppose, on to Christmas dinner tables all over the county.

With the loud gobbling calls still ringing in my ears, I crossed over a narrow humpback bridge which spans the railway line from Dublin to the south, and minutes later reached a corner where the road turned sharp left. Over a low hedge, deep in a cutting, lay the Grand Canal, its still waters glittering and mirroring the sky and the row of lime trees planted along its tow-path. I left the road, scrambled down the steep embankment to the canal's edge, and followed the mucky tow-path towards the village of Sallins. It was a huge relief to be off the tarmac again, after the long stint since Slievethoul, and I delighted in the soft, grass-covered clay surface underfoot, and the quietness of the cutting through which the canal ran.

It is difficult to guess the effect a large group of navigators, as the canal men became known, would have on the quiet rural scene of eighteenth-century Ireland, when they began work on the construction of the Grand Canal. The first sections of canal were, oddly enough, built near Sallins, while long drawn out negotiations on compensation for Dublin city landowners were being completed.

Long before this there were years of debates and lobbying in Dublin and London leading up to the passing of the necessary Parliamentary Acts to enable the project to begin. The general area of the route would have enjoyed a great if brief economic boom as local men and women were recruited to work in the concern, and local farms would have had a considerable boost to the sale of their produce.

Canal technology was in its infancy in Ireland, although much was learned from Britain and France, where works had been under way for years before the Irish canals began. The system depended on the fact that water always flows downwards and finds its level. All you need for a canal to work is a starting point with a supply of water a little higher than the finishing point, and a series of steps or locks to bring the water level down to the finishing point. On the Grand Canal the high point is near Robertstown in County Kildare, just 87m above mean sea level, and the canal steps down west to the Shannon and east to the Liffey in Dublin.

What made the canals revolutionary was the ease by which heavy loads could be transported long distances. It was not economically possible to shift building materials like bricks and stone or quantities metal ores over long distance by road, but it was by water. The coming of the canals opened up Britain and facilitated the distribution of its resources in a way the roads of the time could never achieve.

The original plan for the Grand Canal in Ireland dating back to the beginning of the eighteenth century, was to connect Dublin to the Shannon by linking the rivers Liffey, Rye, Boyne and Brosna. Initial surveys, however, suggested this scheme would be impracticable, and so the alternative of constructing a canal all the way was examined, and various routes surveyed to identify the best. A route suggested by the original chief engineer, Thomas Omer, was selected, and serious survey work began in 1757, followed a year later by the first construction work. The investors knew they were in for the long haul, but even so they must have been taken aback at the apparent lack of progress; the canal only reached Sallins from the mouth of the Liffey in 1780, 22 years after work had begun. It would be another 24 years before the first commercial barge would reach Shannon Harbour from Dublin, in April 1804.

After a short distance along a leafy tow-path I reached Sallins, where the stonework canal harbour, decorated by flowerbeds rimmed by white-painted tractor tyres, was lined with canal craft of all kinds, from gaily-painted barges to dilapidated cruisers, their timbers bleached silver. The harbour is a pleasant place overlooked by two pubs and terraces of well-restored Victorian houses; on a side street is Sallins Catholic church, an unassuming, tin-roofed building with a free-standing belfry. It is a prefabricated building, imported from England and erected here in 1922.

The village of Sallins owes its existence to the Grand

Canal, and is only one of many out-of-the-way places across the midlands which thrived on the commerce the canal brought to them. It was the location for one of the first Canal Hotels, which opened in 1784. Sallins became the processing and distribution hub for the agricultural lands all about it, first as a great flour-milling centre, and subsequently, as agricultural practices changed, meat-processing became the main industry. It has now become a suburb of Dublin, due to being on the rail line to the city.

I crossed over the canal at the hump-backed bridge which carries the road between Clane and Naas; a busy road frequented by huge lorries with tarpaulined loads leaving a trail of dust behind them, the roars of their engines ignored by a dainty and colourful yellow wagtail that sported along the bridge parapet. The western side of the bridge is industrial, and as I descended to the north canal bank I was assailed by the smell and noise emanating from the meat factory. I was happy to speed my pace and follow the tow-path out of the village, disturbing uncountable flock of sparrows which flowed like liquid into the thick thorn hedge bounding the path, and hearing once more the sound of the breeze in the trees, punctuated by the caw-caw-caw of the grey-backed crow.

After a while I passed the junction where the old Corbally extension to Naas from the Grand Canal heads south. Here there is a tiny overgrown island called Soldier's Island, a name that seems to have originated in 1798, when it was briefly garrisoned during the rebellion. The 3km-long Naas link, which has only been dredged infrequently, has led to it becoming a rich aquatic plant habitat and reed bed, acquiring the title 'Area of Scientific Interest'.

The canal wound around now, curving sharply westwards, an alteration made necessary on the advice of General

Vallency, the noted military engineer and antiquary, about how and where the river Liffey should be crossed. Omer had suggested that the canal should be locked down into the Liffey and up again on the other side, and the necessary excavation work had already commenced, signs of which are still visible today. Vallency's recommendation, however, was that an aqueduct should carry the canal over the Liffey some distance upstream, involving two sharp bends on the canal, and his was the solution chosen.

The waters of the Grand along this stretch were very clear and I marvelled at the rich green of the aquatic plants that grew in profusion on the undulating bottom. I stopped and gazed intently into the water in the hope of spotting fish, but instead, on patches where the gravel bottom was free of weed, I spotted a few fresh water crayfish. They were not moving, so it is possible I was looking at the cast-off shells of little green lobsters, as the animal is normally nocturnal. I have seen live ones about 100mm long, and am not surprised that they were once fished actively for eating, like their larger, salt-sea cousins. They were attracted into traps using raw meat as bait, and I am told it was common to collect large baskets of them for sale in the cities. I know that fresh water crayfish are a favourite of the otter, and where they are to be found, otters will also live.

The tow-path was often divided from the canal by a curtain of reeds and bull rushes which rustled quietly in the occasional breeze that disturbed the surface of the canal water, and although I had not seen any so far, I could hear moorhens, often loudly, exchange remarks to one another deep in the reed beds' cover. As I rounded another bend a heron took off from the bank with a complaining squawk, and with slow wing-beats, lifted onto the breeze, a nearby beech tree. It was the first of many I was to see before I reached the Shannon nearly 100km to the west.

After this bend I came to the Liffey aqueduct, which is still an impressive piece of work today, nearly 220 years after it was constructed. The five-arched structure, one of the more spectacular engineering works of our canal system, carries the canal and the tow-path high over the river; on a limestone plaque in Roman lettering is the legend, 'Leinster Aqueduct 1783, R. Evans Engineer'. By this time, 26 years after he had started work on the project, Thomas Omer had fallen out of favour, and a succession of other engineers were to see the canal through to completion.

Swinging around from the aqueduct what looked like an Iron-Age earthworks came into on a low hill to the south, covered with bushes that could be the ancestors of the thorn-bush pallisade that fortified its banks 2,000 years ago. The fields to the side of the canal were thronged with sheep, their great numbers a result, I am sure, of European Union's headage payment system, through which the Union pays farmers not to slaughter, no matter how old or infirm.

Overgrown with brambles at the side of the tow-path I came across a series of concentric stone-built rings, the largest about 4m across, an ingenious safety valve that controls overflow when the canal is in flood. Further on, glimpsed between the hawthorns of the canalside hedge, I spotted Sandymount House, a fine and neat late eighteenth century house. It stands on a hill overlooking the canal and Digby Bridge, named after a local landlord and a Director of the Grand Canal Company. A man I met near the bridge told me that the house was owned by one of the Rolling Stones, who when renovating it a few years ago installed in it, with all the furniture and fittings, a complete Irish pub.

Wrens were plentiful along the canal banks, flitting back and forth between the reeds and the trees bordering the canal. I realised that I had seen a great increase in wildlife activity since I had joined the canal. The canal is a linear oasis for wildlife, a place where the disturbance created by roads and dwellings intrudes only slightly and where modern farmers' 'improvements' and fertiliser do not reach. Apart from common plants such as daisies and dandelions, you can find refugees and escapees, survivors of the plants which filled the 'underdeveloped' countryside at the time of building the canal, over 200 years ago. When you think about it, there are very few such places of asylum remaining in the modern countryside; apart from the little churchyards attached to old or ruined churches, or disused railway embankments. In these places in recent years botanists have been rediscovering rare plants long extinct in the rest of the countryside.

A copse of beech trees provided some welcome variety along the water side, and crossing a stile to enter it, I disturbed a grey squirrel which had been foraging amongst the beech mast. It went bounding off, light as a feather, across the ground and up a tree on the blind side.

I saw from my map that I was approaching the demesne of Landenstown House, and I asked a man coming towards me , wearing a long tattered tweed coat that came over the top of his wellingtons, who lived in the house.

'Is this Landenstown House?' I asked pointing to the demesne walls.

'Well I don't know that, now. You wouldn't know - well I don't know it anyway.' He walked on, continuing to scrutinise me with exaggerated backward glances until he was out of sight around a corner.

After a few minutes I came to an elaborate set of gates, with a sign indicating that it was indeed the entrance to Landenstown Estate. Behind the gates, on either side of the entrance driveway, were two neat doll's house gate lodges, with limestone pillared porticos and diamond paned windows. I knocked on one of the doors and asked the woman who answered if it would be okay to go up the avenue to take a photograph of the house.

'Quite a few goes up there,' she said. 'I don't think they would say anything to you.'

She told me that Germans owned the place, but did not live there all year round. A farm manager ran the farm for them.

So I walked up the mile-long avenue and out of the trees into a broad rolling parkland. Landenstown House, an unusual five-bayed, gable-fronted building with projecting wings, stood at the edge of a wood. Its red front door set in a granite portico was the only decorative element of what was a carefully proportioned, simple façade. I approached to within a couple of hundred yards of the house but I was deterred from going further by the sight of an Alsatian dog, on a long tether, eyeing me silently. So I took my photos from a distance, and reluctantly returned back down the avenue to meet the canal again.

After the lock gates beyond Landenstown the Grand Canal has reached its summit; the next lock, over five miles on, is the first of eighteen that gradually reduce the canal levels in steps until the River Shannon is reached. The main supply of water to the canal comes from the Pollardstown Fen near the village of Robertstown, my destination for the day.

Pollardstown Fen is one of the finest examples of a fen in Ireland, 225 hectares of marshland fed by the subterranean waters of the gravel beds under the Curragh of Kildare. A typical fen consists of a shallow body of water fed by springs and streams. Over time the reed and sedge beds around the perimeter spread to form a skin over most of the surface, and eventually as the live and dead vegetation builds up, the fen becomes a raised peat bog. While the fen exists it is extremely rich in plant species, with up to 200 varieties compared to the 150 in a species-rich raised peat bog. Pollardstown, which has the largest area in Europe of sedge, is now under the protection of Duchas, the Heritage Council.

I followed the canal now through a cutting and a look at my map confirmed that it was passing along the northern flanks of a low eminence called the Hill of Downings. On each bank of the canal there were overgrown, scooped-out, quarry-like excavations which I later learned were the sites of good deposits of the dense clays which were used to form a waterproof layer lining the bottom of the canal. Apparently clay is still taken from here to repair breaches. Along this stretch the water seemed stiller and even clearer than before, its surface still decorated with the remaining plates of the season's water lilies, and from the tow-path raised a metre above the water, thick patches of Canadian pond-weed rising vertically from the bottom looked like a miniature coniferous forest.

As I emerged from the cutting, the low shapes of Dunmurray Hill and Grange Hill came into view to the south west. The surrounding country dropped away as the canal, atop a rampart now, swung around towards the village of Robertstown. The terracotta pile of the old canal hotel beckoned me on to the picturesque village, which has changed little since commercial traffic ceased to use the canals in the early 1960s. The great hotel was unfortunately looking a little the worse for wear. A plaque on its façade recalled its

more recent heyday, stating that it received a European Architectural Heritage award in 1975. This hotel looks a little out-of-scale with it's neighbours today, so imagine how impressive it must have looked when it was built towards the end of the eighteenth century, when, besides the canal stores nearby, its only companions would have been a few sod-roofed mud cabins. It was built, together with others at Shannon Harbour, Tullamore Harbour, Sallins, and

Portobello Harbour in Rathmines, to cater for the tourists and travelling merchants that the Grand Canal Company expected to avail of the new cross-country route provided by the canal. The hotels at Sallins and Tullamore are long since demolished, Shannon Harbour is an ivy-covered ruin while Robertstown, only a tiny percentage of its accommodation in use as a visitor's centre and a restaurant in season, awaits a significant boom in canal usage. Only Portobello survives and thrives with a secure future; it was beautifully restored in the early 1980s, as the centrepiece of a private third-level college. It was described in an 1821 guide-book as 'a very fine edifice ... It has in front a very fine portico, and the interior is fitted up with great elegance for the accommodation of families and single gentlemen. The beauty and salubrity of the situation, enlivened by the daily arrival and departure of the canal boats, render it a truly delightful summer residence'.

Early passengers on the canal travelled in 'flyboats', barges towed by teams of fast horses which were frequently changed, and achieving average speeds of 12km per hour, including negotiating locks, so the top speed could have been anything up to 20km per hour. They carried 50 First Class and 35 Second Class passengers and were like floating inns, with food and drink served, and card-games, singing, and all kinds of jollity taking place during long journeys. An account written in 1844 of a journey by flyboat gives an indication of the efficiency and speed of the craft:

The horses were put to, and away they went at full gallop exactly at seven o'clock. But the locks on the first ten or fifteen miles are very numerous, though it must be confessed they passed through them with wonderful rapidity. They will get through a double lock even on the ascent in five minutes, and on the descent towards the Shannon in three minutes or less. The dress of the postilions, the measured canter or gallop of the horses, the vibrations of the rope, the swell that precedes the boat, and the dexterity with which the men and horses dive under the arches of the bridges without for a moment slackening their pace, all produce a very curious and picturesque scene such as I have never seen equalled in Holland on any of its canals.

For about 60 years from their inauguration in the late eighteenth century the flyboats were instrumental in opening up the lands beyond the Shannon to large numbers of travellers; in 1846, 120,615 passengers were carried.

I was pleased that the rain which had been threatening all afternoon delayed its arrival until I was walking along the quayside past Robertstown House, giving me an excellent excuse to turn into one of the little pubs that adorns the village. Ordering a pint at the bar, I exchanged pleasantries with the only customer, an ageless, brown faced man in an oily donkey jacket, hunched over the formica bar as if paying homage to the half empty pint in front of him.

'Are ye out on a stroll, are ye?' he asked, swivelling around on his stool to face me. I said I had walked from Sallins, and his curiosity roused, he launched into a series of questions to confirm I was not having him on.

He asked me had I passed Landenstown House.

'Sure it's a German that owns it, Beckmann is his name. It's a long way you've come then,' he said, apparently satisfied with my claim. 'This is the highest point of the canal you're on now. The second step of the hotel was level with the top of Nelsons pillar in Dublin, when it was there. The survey was done years ago, and that's what they said. That's why they call this the summit level. Once you go to the nineteenth lock at Lowtown, you're fallin' both ways then, down to the Shannon and back to Dublin.'

I ordered a pint from the barman, a young lad sitting on a stool behind the bar reading a newspaper, and offered one to the other customer, which he accepted.

As our pints were poured and served, I enjoyed the conversation which gently flowed, in the way that all good pub conversations do, through diverse subjects like the difference between Irish miles and English miles, the banquets they used to have at the old hotel, and a tidy thatched cottage I had seen on the other side of the canal.

'Did you notice the golden colour of the thatch?' he asked as he finished his old pint and raised the new one to me. When I said I had admired the colour, he said. 'It's because it's made from oaten straw. Ye can't get it around here now, he had to go to Athy to get it. The combines break it all up but the old steam mills used to let the complete stalk through the drum. They still have a few places around Athy and Portlaoise where they do it the old way.'

Eventually we got to talking about the old days on the canals, because it turned out that he spent much of his younger life on the barges, travelling between Lowtown and Dublin, and west to Tullamore and the Shannon. They went all the way down through Dublin to Ringsend, and would load off the seagoing ships, cargoes of buck wheat, 50 tons per barge.

'The cost of shipping was £1-6s a ton, no matter whether you were going a few miles or all the way to Limerick,' he told me.

I asked him if it was a good life.

'It was good as a young fella, ah it was, but it was a rough ould life in the hard weather. You stayed on the ould barge as long as ye were travellin'. One winter there was ice on the canal for upwards of six weeks, and ye couldn't move at all, even with the fifteen horsepower engine. We spent a long time taking turf from a Bord na Mona place in Offaly, down to a depot beside Harolds Cross Bridge, where there's an army barracks up agin it.

'Some barges were carrying Guinness down to Ballinasloe and Limerick. 170 tons of Guinness a day used to pass be here! One of them got lost down on Lough Derg in November 1946, in a storm, ye know. Dem boats, they were flat bottomed, with no keel or anything. They shouldn't have been out on the lough in that weather but they didn't want to be stuck in some village with a little harbour and no life along the way. They wanted to be down in Killaloe where the dances would be goin' on an' all that. There was three drowned, and one survived. And another man swam and got to the shore, but he was exhausted, and there was no one to help him, and he died of exposure. The barge sank in 300 feet of water.'

We observed a respectful few moments silence as we took long draughts from our pints. The chat moved on to how the Guinness barrels being carried by the barges could explode on a hot summer's day, the hoops of the barrel parting with a loud bang, and the drink pouring out across the deck. Fear of this and, of course, a love of Guinness and a horror of waste led to the barge men taking their own precautions on hot thirsty days, by drilling a hole in a barrel and releasing the pressure by bleeding off a couple of pints!

'You wouldn't go too hard on it, an auld pint or two would be enough. A fellow I know was takin' a load down to Rahan, jam and every class o' thing, with all kinds of groceries. There was no beer on it, only this cask so he said he'd sample this, and it was altar wine. He got a jug o' this and of course he drank it. Well he was as sick as a dog, and it took him three days to get over it! An' he said it must have been some sermons that priest was giving!'

After a few more stories, my companion finished his pint with a very final gesture, and looking at the clock, reluctantly bade me good luck and headed out the door.

While I do not mind walking in the rain, much of the enjoyment of a walking journey, the countryside, the flora and fauna, the views, the pleasure of picnicing and pausing to speak to people along the way, depend on at least a few good spells of weather – constant rain prohibits all of these. The weather over the next while was dismal, forcing me to take a break from my trek, and then things got busy in 'real life', bringing other demands on my free time. Before I could cobble together any more opportunities, winter was too advanced to get days that were long enough, and I reluctantly put my *Bay to Bay* project on hold for a few months until the following spring. I had completed almost 80km, more than one-quarter of what I expected the total cross-country journey to add up to between Dublin Bay and Galway Bay.

GALWAY COUNTY LIBRARIES

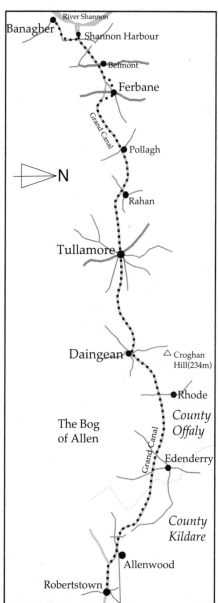

PART TWO

SPRING:
Robertstown
to
Edenderry

From Robertstown to Edenderry, County Offaly

A weak March sun was doing its best to warm the land when I set out from Robertstown a few months later to resume my cross-Ireland pedestrian tour. My next goal was the County Offaly town of Edenderry, and leaving a sleepy Robertstown behind, I crossed Binn's Bridge and set out west-wards along the glass-still waters of the canal once again.

Not far out of Robertstown I passed two canal branches which connect the Grand to the Barrow line, which, using the Barrow River, has a tow-path that can be followed all the way to the ancient hamlet of St Mullins in south County Carlow, about twenty miles north of Waterford Harbour. I had considered at an early stage heading southwest along the Barrow line to Rathangan and Monasterevin, which I had walked before, and then turning west for Portarlington, Mountmellick and Rosenalis so that I could include the Slieve Bloom Mountains on the route to the west. I would then get to Portumna by way of Kinnity and Birr. Painstaking exami-nation of the maps, however, and a reconnaissance on the ground showed that for the sake of a few miles in the wooded hills of the Slieve Bloom, I would have to take the route along many miles of road, some of it boring and often hazardous.

Farther on I passed the nineteenth lock, the first of seventeen which lower the water level to that of the Shannon. Beyond a beautifully-kept lock-keepers cottage I reached the mini-harbour of Lowtown, once a coal depot associated by way of the Barrow Line with the coal mines at Castlecomer in County Kilkenny, and providing stabling for the many trace horses, the great animals that pulled the canal barges before they became mechanised. Here the water's edge was lined with barges, boats, launches and cruisers of every conceivable shape, size and colour. Apart from the larger craft, many were clearly home-made, and some, it seemed clear, built from memory after the instructions, if indeed there had been any, had been lost. There were floating, sawn-off caravans with asbestos chimneys, barely floating spacecraft and some constructions which looked decidedly unstable. There was not a soul around the place keeping an eye on this fantasy fleet, but there was not much here worth stealing!

I continued along the north bank and over the narrow but swift flowing Slate river. Rivers, at one time such an important feature of the landscape for communications, drainage, irrigation and a source of food, seem of little consequence in the minds of most people today. Nobody travels by river any more, drainage and irrigation are matters that only interest the declining numbers of farmers, and with the exception of leisure angling, rivers do not feature today as a source of food. As we travel by road, river crossings are often unnoticed, and at 60 miles per hour we miss the myriad of smaller but not insignificant streams which are culverted under the highways. Curious about the waters which flowed beneath my feet and the canal here with such vigour, I later followed on ordnance maps the course of the Slate to trace its route. I found that it rises north west of the village of Prosperous in County Kildare, collects a series of smaller drainage streams as it flows westwards, water which might otherwise have, but from some slight obstruction in this low-lying landscape, flowed into the Liffey a few kilometres away and ended up in the Irish sea. Instead, it is taken southwestwards by the Slate through the town of Rathangan, where, joined with the Figile and the Cushina, it becomes the Black river. This in turn flows into the great Barrow north of Monasterevin, and so, water from springs in the peat near Prosperous finally reach the Celtic Sea and the Atlantic by way of Waterford Harbour after a journey of nearly 150 km.

Up to my right now was the village of Allenwood, a scatter of bungalows along the Rathangan to Clane road, each with its dark-brown stack of turf at the rear. Turf-cutting has always been a way-of-life here and is the reason for Allenwood's existence. Its heyday as a turf centre is past, however, having reached its high point in 1934, when the first National Turf-Cutting Championships were held here, and later when it had one of the first turf-sod burning electricity generating stations, contributing what was at the time a significant 40 megawatts to the national grid when it was built in 1952. By the 1990s the plant was obsolete, however, and it was closed in 1994.

At the next canal bridge, a strange oblique-arched structure called locally the Skew Bridge, because it is the only bridge crossing the canal at an angle, I crossed over to the south bank, which seemed to have a better tow-path. I was following the canal away from the road network, and the air became quieter for a while as the surrounding land dropped gently away and the canal flowed along an earthen rampart.

Before long, I passed Bord na Mona's Peat Briquette factory, all tubes and chimneys, as the canal took me out into open country. I was gradually leaving behind the good agricultural land of Kildare, and passing into an area of raised bogs, between which were poorly drained green fields reclaimed when turf was cut in former times.

At Ticknevin bridge and lock I got my first extensive view of Ireland's great central boglands, the Bog of Allen. To the west, the north west and south west extended a flat, dark landscape scattered with scrub trees and occasional extensive blankets of coniferous forest. In the distance a water-tower piercing the horizon pinpointed the location of the town of Edenderry, just over the border in County Offaly. Over to the right I could see Carbury Hill, where the river Boyne rises. I could just make out the ruin of a tall-chimneyed fortified house which crowns the summit, built in the late sixteenth century by the Cowley family, ancestors of the Duke of Wellington.

Everyone who went to school as I did in the 1950s will be familiar with the Bog of Allen. We learned that Ireland was shaped like a saucer with mountains all round the edge and the middle of the saucer was the Bog of Allen. We were never told just who Allen was, and in spite of some research I am still no wiser. Well, here it was, once a vast raised bog lying 70 or 80m above sea level with a scattering of small hills 20 or 30m higher. Many, such as Walshe's Island and Derryhinch, are still called 'islands' in their placenames, harking back hundreds if not thousands of years, when they island settlements on a landscape much wetter than today, linked by primitive toghers or bog roads made of tree trunks. In recent years a number of these bog paths, of Bronze Age date and possibly earlier, have been exposed at the bottom of peat cuttings across the Bog of Allen, indicating that there must have been a considerable population in the area at the time and a significant level of commerce between settlements. The bogs and the routes across them are frequently mentioned in the old annals, mainly because they were militarily important; foreign raiders of monastic centres from the Pale around Dublin or from the east or west coasts, unfamiliar with the area, often found themselves 'bogged' down and vulnerable to counter-attack, or forced into lethal bottlenecks on toghers. In 1395 a party of English marauders retreating eastwards out of Offaly were caught up with the Offaly chief O'Conor on 'the causeway of Cruachain, where great numbers of them were slain, and 60 horses taken from them', according to the *Annals of Ireland*. Most of the old toghers only went out of use in the seventeenth century, when the important ones were replaced by permanent roads.

Again I followed the canal out along an earthen embankment, this one a massive 8m-high construction nearly 7km long across a roadless, uninhabited wilderness of bog and scrub. It was the construction of this section which nearly brought the whole Grand Canal venture to a premature end in the 1780s. Every load of clay they brought in to build the embankment sank without trace into what seemed to be a bottomless bog. Eventually, after ten years when the company was close to giving up, the bog's appetite was finally satisfied, and a stable embankment was achieved.

At Ticknevin the water of the canal has reached a level which is maintained for almost twenty miles before having to lock down again. Obviously, the less locks there are on a canal, the faster barges can travel. The disadvantage, however, was when a breach occurred on such a stretch, an awful lot of water would be lost, and a lot of flooding would take place before the section was emptied. This has happened here on a number of occasions over the last 200 years, the worst instance in 1985 near Edenderry when 60 million gallons emptied into the surrounding countryside, a disaster it took more than a year to completely repair. Ticknevin lock was tastefully landscaped with planters and flowers, and I sat a while to enjoy a picnic of chicken sandwiches and a glass of full-bodied Rioja before setting out again out for Edenderry.

The surroundings on both sides of the long, straight canal were wonderfully wild and seemed almost untouched by man. Pheasants could be heard nearby, and on a few occasions I disturbed snipe, water hens and teal. The tow-path was quite overgrown and had reduced to a comfortable trail that wound its way sometimes close to the water and sometimes along the outer edge of the high embankment. Dragonflies hawked on the still air along the reed beds, taking little notice of me as they droned by like tiny model aircraft. While I could identify only a few plants such as meadowsweet and water mint, they, like the majority of wild flowers, had not yet blossomed in March but it was clear that in early summer this place would be stocked with a riot of colourful blossoms, attracting clouds of insects and butterflies, which in turn would be attracting their aerial predators. But for the moment all was still, a kind of a lull, as nature composed herself and worked behind the scenes for the next great thrust; this spring quiet must have led the Romans to dedicate 19 February to Tacita, the goddess of silence. Although it was well into March, I could still sense the silence lying heavily on the air, the expectation in the shrubs and plants whose buds hung full and ready for the expected moment. If one listens hard enough on these quiet days, one can sense the hum of the boundless power held in check in all nature, awaiting the signal to burst gloriously forth in a colourful re-birth.

As I reached a coniferous wood that had formed the horizon since leaving Ticknevin Lock, the canal veered left and reached silverly into the distance to the west, as far as the eye can see. At the western edge of the wood, I walked out of County Kildare and into County Offaly.

Offaly, described in a tourist brochure as 'undiscovered country', is just that. The fact that only short stretches of two main routes radiating from Dublin to provincial centres pass through the county has helped to continue as a little-known part of Ireland. It is not a rich county today, but it must have been important centuries ago: Offaly has more early Christian monastic centres than most other parts of Ireland. Later, the existence of the two great ancient highways, the Shannon River on its western border, and the Esker Riada on the north must have given the county a strategic importance. The lands of the county not under bog were rich enough to attract English colonisers in the sixteenth century when Offaly and neighbouring Laois were planted in the reign of Mary, after the bloody campaigns of destruction of most local Irish clans. Laois was named Queen's County and Offaly King's County in honour of Mary and her husband, Philip of Spain, and what is Daingean today was named Philipstown, which remained until the early twentieth century, when the county name reverted to Offaly. Today much of the county is prosperous with fine, well-laid out towns like Tullamore and Birr, each with a rich store of well-preserved Georgian buildings and public spaces, a legacy of their former English owners. But in spite of the cultural and historical riches it does possess, Offaly has never been seriously marketed, and is not a well-known Irish tourist destination, probably one of the reasons I like the place so much.

Edenderry came into view again, with the ruins of Blundell's Castle and a church tower joining the water tower on the skyline. The Blundell Aqueduct, which takes the canal over the Rathangan to Edenderry road, is next to a small white house at the end of this straight. Here I came across a large herd of feral goats feeding on the embankment. They were all sizes and ages, the older ones with long scraggy coats and weird curling horns, the very young quite frisky, like new-born lambs. They took no notice of me however, and even posed patiently as I took a few photographs.

I carried on to reach the branch of the feeder canal to Edenderry, crossed by a very quaint and elegant 4ft-wide horse bridge, and I followed the feeder to Edenderry harbour, a pleasant pool on the south side of the town.

Edenderry grew up around Blundell's Castle, the ruins of which dominate the town; it was sacked and 'slighted' by King James' army in 1691. It was built in the sixteenth century by the Cooley family, and was one of many castles and mottes in this area, outposts of the English Pale. The distinctive mound of a Norman motte occupies a nearby hilltop to the south of the town, built in the centre of a much older tree-planted earthen ringfort, its shape clearly visible from the canal bank in wintertime when the surrounding trees are leafless.

Edenderry's main street consists of two terraces of sturdy Victorian houses and shops. leading to a square with a fine granite-faced market house. Some of the excellent fanlighted doorways must date to the early nineteenth century, particularly those east of the square; in 1830, according to the historian Samuel Lewis, Edenderry contained '214 houses, well built of stone and slated; ... well paved and supplied with

water... it is rapidly improving'. It is one of those typical Irish country towns or large villages based on a main street which develops organically like a skin on either side of the road; but behind the street, framed frequently through the stable entries of the nineteenth-century buildings, glimpses of the green and open countryside beyond are presented, as if the buildings are but the film set of a pretend town.

On the Main Street is a gateway flanked by two stone piers inscribed with the date 1840, and topped with magnificent bronze stag's heads. The gateway leads by a leafy avenue called the Church Walk to Castropetre Church and churchyard. Near the end of the avenue on a plinth stands a statue by the sculptor Joseph Kirk of Arthur Blundell, the third Marquess of Downshire, founder of the modern town. Besides the 14,000 acres of land around Edenderry, the Downshires owned other large tracts of land in the nineteenth century, particularly in County Wicklow, where Blundell also founded the town of Blessington. He is said to have been a good landlord, and although politically a conservative, he involved himself in the improvement of his tenantry and in the establishment of schools on his estates.

The graveyard has an interesting array of funerary monuments; the names and dates tell the history and background of the landed gentry and the considerable Protestant community of the area. Sadly on many, the last inscription commemorates sons who gave their lives in the First World War.

I had a quiet night in Edenderry, enjoying a good meal, followed by a nightcap in Kavanagh's pub opposite the market house. The wall behind the bar in the pub had panelling of such good quality that I had to ask about it, to be told that in a former life it had been part of the choir stalls in a monastery in County Cork!

From Edenderry to Tullamore,
County Offaly

I left Edenderry at 9.30 the following morning, and returning to the Grand Canal set off westwards following the north bank; it was a guess as to which was the better side to follow, and in this case the north looked well trodden so I took a chance. It was a fine day but with little sunshine in evidence, but although the forecast was for gales and rain from the west, there were no signs in the western sky of such conditions. I often notice that the forecasters, in spite of all the technology available to them, can get the timing wrong, and I hoped to be comfortably ensconced in my next destination, Daingean, before the weather deteriorated.

A short distance outside Edenderry I crossed a bridge to the south side, following a sign for Daingean 19km away. I had not progressed far when I caught sight of an animal sliding out of the canal 30m ahead, disturbing a heron which took off with indignant squawks. It must have been an otter, who slid smoothly into the canalside undergrowth and out of sight. I remembered when I previously walked this section of canal the tow-path had been littered with fresh-water clam shells, which an angler had told me was a sign that otters were about, although on that occasion I saw none. It was the first of a number of sightings of otters I was to have over the next few days. The heron, with its great plank-like wings and retractable neck, is one of my favourite birds and is plentiful on the canals; a pair nest near my suburban home in Dublin, and almost every morning at breakfast I watch them laboriously leave the trees and head for the nearby river to start the day's fishing.

I came upon the grass-covered Rathmor Bridge, over the canal with no road leading to it from either side; there may have been 200 years ago, but the need for it must have gone and now the fields covered it. I stood awhile on the bridge, serenaded by a cacophony of wrens in the bushes, looking about for the rath of 'Rathmore', but in vain. A little farther on I came across a granite milepost, the first I had noticed on the canal bank; it had been pushed over, probably by cattle using it as a scratching stone, and part of the stone which had been under the ground was as fresh as if it had been carved only yesterday. The upper surface, covered with yellow, grey, black and green lichens, had the number 30 incised into it, presumably indicating that Dublin was 30 Irish miles to the east.

Near Cartland Bridge I came across an emaciated-looking young man of about 25 sitting on a tiny stool at the canal's edge, fishing. I asked him if there were much to be had here and he quickly replied there was not, but went on the say that tench, pike and bream were plentiful further down!

Featureless stretches of canal can prolong the journey, and although this was a pleasant section on a tow-path of comfortable grassy sward, it was quite boring. After another half-an-hour, however, it was with relief that I recognised Crohan Hill coming into view, peeking over the horizon ahead. Reaching 150m above sea level, it is the only high point for many miles, an isolated outcrop of basalt which forced its way up through the limestone bedrock aeons ago. The changing profile of that hill was to become very familiar for many miles of my journey, and it would not sink below the horizon until I entered the town of Tullamore the following afternoon.

The skyscape was magnificent now, a pageant of sculpted clouds on the dark base of the landscape, featureless but for a line of electricity pylons a long way away marching off towards the south. This is perhaps one of the loneliest parts of the Grand Canal, a real wilderness where one feel civilisation is remote. The very isolation of the place, a primordial landscape of scrub and patches of coniferous forestry crossed by a myriad of drainage ditches, must provide a safe habitat for many of Ireland's species of animal and bird. The last time I had passed here I had seen, among the more common birds, a pair of buzzards, rare in any part of Ireland other than the Antrim coast.

I passed along the edge of a dense, and dark coniferous wood, the outer trees of which were covered with a thick layer of green moss, and continued along a straight stretch of canal that brought me to Rhode bridge. Here you can see the deep polished grooves worn in the limestone quoins of the canal bridge, rope marks left by the many thousands of horses towing barges that had passed this way over the previous century and a half. A sign at the bridge advertised Mulvin's pub in Rhode as serving 'great Guinness in a pleasant atmosphere'. Unfortunately Rhode was not part of my itinerary for the day, and I kept going.

After passing the spectacular and substantial ruins of Toberdaly House on a hill to the north, I passed out into a wide open landscape of black bog, on a tow-path which trembled beneath my feet as I walked along, despite the fact that it was high above the bog surface.

This bog, as a source of fuel, is nearing the end of its useful life, and soon will be added to the 85,000 hectares of harvested bog in the possession of Bord na Mona; indeed, by the year 2030 it is likely there will be no peat left in Ireland to provide fuel. What is to become of this huge land resource is something that has been argued at many levels in Ireland for a long time. The economies of County Offaly and to a lesser extent County Kildare have been sustained over the last 50 years by the harvesting of peat from the vast bogs that lie across them, and the people who have worked the bogs are concerned what is to happen when the peat is exhausted. Throughout the 1980s and 1990s many research projects have been carried out on alternative uses for what are called 'cutaway' bogs. Agricultural crops have been planted and assessed, experiments carried out on the development of vast areas of grassland, and the viability of planting quick-growing forestry as a replacement fuel have been examined.

On the canal bank beside a tiny deserted cottage, its garden overgrown with rhododendrons, I sat to eat a banana. I was entertained by a grey wagtail displaying to his mate at the far side of the canal; the male is a spectacularly beautiful bird, with a black beard, grey back, black barred wings, white under-tail and a startling yellow breast. Preening, he spread out the white-tipped grey feathers of his long tail, and spraying them around in all directions, twisted them up like a contortionist. His mate, with plumage a little paler and with no black markings, perched on the edge of the canal and took no notice. I had to drag myself away.

The canal veered around towards Crohan Hill, and by

now the cairn crowning the summit of the hill was visible, an old graveyard reaching up its slopes. Crohan, 'the green mound of Cruachan' was an important place in days gone by, and the ceremonial clan meeting place of the O'Conors up until the mid-seventeenth century.

A water tower appeared gradually over the horizon ahead suggesting that Daingean was not much further on. Nearby I spotted the first person since leaving Edenderry, a man attended by a dog, pottering about with a sleán at an obscure task in a field below us, dressed in wellingtons, long black overcoat and tweed cap. He saw me approaching and, giving me a hearty wave, walked ahead to intercept me for a chat. His dog sniffed enthusiastically at my feet to chart my past few hours, and as I stooped to pat him, his master told me proudly that the little foxhound was ten years old and a great companion. I asked him if this was the part of the canal called 'The Red Women'.

'"The Red Girls", yeah,' he replied. I asked about the story behind the name.

'The boatmen christened it that. There were three or four red-haired girls in it years ago, the time of the barges, who lived below near the drawbridge,' he pointed off to where we had come from.

'In the little cottage with the rhododendrons?' I asked.

'No, beyont, about three perches, the house was there, I remember it was an ould house when Bord na Mona came.'

'They must have been good-looking girls?' I asked.

'Seeming they were the Red Girls,' he replied, 'what county man are you, if ye don't mind me askin'?'

I told him I was from Waterford and he said, after a moment's thought, 'there is a relation of a man up here named Mick Crowley there, would ye know him?'

I told him I did not, that Waterford was a big place. I went on to ask him if he knew any of the stories about Crohan Hill.

'I don't know much about it but St Brigid is supposed to have received her veil in the old church that used to be on the hill, and St Patrick was there as well, and left the mark of his horse's hoof where he took a leap onto the hilltop.'

He seemed satisfied that he had checked me out, and with a 'good luck, now', went back with his dog to continue his work.

A little farther on, as I passed a cottage beside the canal, a woman came out to say hello.

'Are ye from around?' she asked.

I told her I had come from Dublin and was walking to Banagher.

'Oh are ye? You're great – that's a terrible walk! Have you a boat or a car?'

I told her no. I asked her would it be possible to have a glass of water, as my water bottle was empty.

'Of course you can, love,' she said and she went inside to get one. She returned with a great mug of water and said, 'That's real spring water, the likes of which ye wouldn't get in Dublin, I'll warrant.'

It was good and I told her so. She seemed inordinately pleased at my compliment, and after thanking her again, I set off. A moment or so later a sandy brown hare with white tips to his ears leaped up ahead of me giving me a fright and bounded off into the canal-side hedge at speed. When I looked back the woman was still there, a smile on her face, and she watched me go until I passed out of sight.

I was disappointed to pass the water tower that I had been walking towards for some time, as I thought it was in

Daingean. A spire, however, in the near distance, and a golf course under construction suggested I was at last coming close to the town. As the canal swung around to the right I heard the noise of traffic, and shortly after, the Edenderry to Daingean road joined the canal, keeping me company for the last kilometre into town. Reynold's Bar, the Sportsmans Inn beckoned, and although it was after 3pm I went in to see if they could give me a late lunch. Roast was still hot, and I was served up a trencherman's meal of beef, potatoes, cabbage and carrots, piled high on the plate. As I was trying to make an impression on this meal for two, the concerned barman came back and asked 'Did you get enough?'

After my late lunch, to which the barman had insisted on adding a bowl of trifle and charged little for the lot, I set off for a walk around the town. Daingean owes its existence to Mary Tudor, who restored Catholicism to England for the period of her reign. She married Philip of Spain, who was later to lead the Inquisition, and confiscating much of what are now the counties of Offaly and Laois, began the 'plantations' of loyal subjects which her successor Elizabeth continued. A great earthen-walled fort was built at Daingean where Philip of Spain is said to have stayed at one stage; all that remains of it, a few bramble-covered mounds of earth, can be found in the fields near the town. The locals told me that there were cellars still in existence underneath, but that may be a local legend.

The main street had many houses that curiously leaned out or back, due, I suppose, to the peaty ground on which they had been built, and little seemed to have changed since the photograph I had seen on the wall of the pub taken almost 100 years before. I soon found the courthouse which was designed by James Gandon, an undistinguished building with a couple of urns on the roof parapet to set it apart. As I walked into the old graveyard next door there was a scurry of workmen who had probably been having a smoke, and in seconds they were looking busy digging and generally pottering about. When they decided I wasn't a European Commission inspector they relaxed again and were chatty and informative. They were part of a 'community work scheme', involved in repairs to walls and paths, cleaning up the graveyard. They very proudly brought me down to where a little stream was flowing past, and showed me a stone and concrete bridge they had built 'all by ourselves'. They had inscribed the names of all involved in the concrete work.

They pointed out the grave of Bishop Charles Dodgeson; one of them said he was the grandfather of Sir Walter Scott, and another disagreed strongly, saying he was the grandfather of Lewis Carroll. A third said he mustn't have been liked hereabouts anyway for he died after he was shot in the street. They also told me of Lord Norbury, a 'hanging judge' who used sit in the courthouse and would fall asleep on the bench. On awakening he was likely to sentence the poor defendant who happened to be before him at the time to death for stealing a chicken. The prisoner would be taken straight across to where the post office now is and hanged.

In spite of resolutions I had made, the Sportsmans Inn drew me in again that evening after I had checked into my Bed and Breakfast. I was late to bed and didn't start out the following morning until after 10am. The day was bright and clear and I looked forward to an easy walk of 15km to Tullamore. I passed the tall grey walls of Daingean Reformatory, their severity and height evidence of their purpose to keep people in; today they perform the same purpose in keeping people out, because the buildings are now used as a storage facility by the National Museum.

St Conleth's Reformatory School was opened in 1870 and was run by the Oblate brothers. With a staff of twenty, it had accommodation for 350 boys under sixteen years of age. The 'inmates' were boys who had been convicted of crimes larceny, housebreaking, vagrancy or assault; they were incarcerated for anything up to four years.

Not far out of Daingean I came to a cottage with a beautiful heather garden facing south onto the canal. A man was working in the garden and I paused to compliment him on it.

'Are you on a walking tour?' he asked.

I told him I was walking to Banagher, and he wanted to know if it was a sponsored walk. This is something I have found a lot in areas where people are not familiar with 'walkers' – they cannot imagine walking long distances for pleasure and assume it must be some kind of strenuous marathon engaged in for charity. I told him I was doing it for fun, and asked him did he remember when the reformatory was open.

'Indeed and I do,' he said, 'the museum keep a lot of artifacts in there now, I believe. They have had open days I never went into it, although as a young lad I was in and out a lot. You'd go in to see the pictures with the lads on a Sunday; they would be issued with a few fags, and we would swop something with them for a smoke. It was great fun.'

'How many were in there then?' I asked.

'I wouldn't be sure, 100 or more I suppose. Some of them were real toughs, but most were okay, very lonely for their families and friends.'

As I progressed away from Daingean the low rolling shapes of the Slieve Bloom Mountains came into view across the flat lands to the south west. Crohan Hill was still in view behind, giving a sense of the distance I was covering. Near another ruined cottage a great bank of daffodils was in bloom, looking startlingly bright against the greyness of the surroundings. I wondered just how long ago the cottier's wife had planted those bulbs to brighten up her little garden in springtime.

The surrounding landscape now consisted of black raised bog on the south side of the canal, while over to the north it was still an untouched wilderness scattered with poor copses of birch and ash. Now and then there were little cottages beside the canal, some derelict but others well looked after; one I passed was a beauty, with a thatched roof and black-and-white decorated quoins, surrounded by a trimmed hedge of mixed shrubs. Picturesquely scattered about the haggard at the side of the cottage were six ancient derelict cars, each one older and more overgrown than the next. Some appeared to be in use as chicken houses, providing great security against foxes, and another was in use as a greenhouse.

As on the previous couple of days, the more remote the countryside the richer the wildlife, the birdlife in particular. I disturbed a flock of about 100 golden plovers, which were grazing along the grassy tow-path. They took off spectacularly in a flowing formation with an easily audible whoosh of wings, leaving a chorus of plaintive, curlew-like calls hanging on the still air. As I stood they wheeled around like a single live thing and, showing their pale undersides and then their brown backs, landed again a little further along. I continued walking and before long, disturbed them again. Off they went once more, this time higher and higher, and after wheeling a few times seemed to set off for the bog to the south, calling all the while. Soon the flock settled into a long crescent, leaders at the centre, and with a few stragglers where the string of a bow might be. Then as I watched, the stragglers made a 180 degree turn, and no sooner were they on a heading to return to the canal than the rest of the flock poured around effortlessly to follow them. They swept past me with a rush of wingbeats heading north, and shortly after having re-formed an arc, the same thing happened, the stragglers, who were the original leaders, turning back, drawing the rest with them. This practise was continued as I watched. They seemed to become obsessed with their aerobatic gyrations and in no hurry to land again, and as they eventually moved away to the east and became a blurred, moving, ghost-like form against the backdrop of the sky I walked on, still hearing their calls for long after.

At Ballycommon Bridge the bright yellow gable of a pub advertised welcome and refreshment, and for once I decided that I had time to spare, only to find the premises was closed. I walked on to reach the long-disused Kilbeggan branch line of the canal, which was built in the 1820s to connect the distillery town of Kilbeggan, 15km to the north, into the system. The contractor was William Dargan, who was to make his name and fortune some years later in the development of the first railway in Ireland, between Dublin and Dun Laoghaire; this contract caused him a lot of difficulty, however, and it took six years to complete the work to the canal company's satisfaction. The Kilbeggan line, however, survived until it was closed and drained in 1961.

Soon after, I reached the twenty-first lock of the Grand Canal, and the first lock since before Edenderry at Ticknevin; it was like meeting a long-lost friend, and I was relieved to see again the black and white woodwork and hear the sound of the gushing water flowing down into the lock, something which had punctuated my journey along the canal up until Ticknevin . Nearby was a towering telecommunications mast that I had first seen some distance back, a red and white steel framework held in position by a dense web of bracing wires; it looked completely alien in this rural setting. The lock keeper told me, in a marvellous Offaly accent, that it was a relay transmitter for Telefís Éireann, and that it 'swayed tirty fuh' in the wind sometimes.

The canal seemed to be descending rapidly towards the west now; after no lock for so many miles I passed a couple in quick succession before reaching a pleasant, grassy stretch with long views south to the Slieve Blooms. A dark grey bank of cloud moved across the horizon ahead, and in the eerie light that ensued, a flock of lapwings rose from the fields to the north of the canal, their ridiculous wings flapping in unison, and under them, in almost exact imitation, a flock of starlings. The two clouds of birds swooped and rose in fluid motion, before settling once again in the fields. Lapwings have always been a characteristic of winter in the midlands, and I have a great fondness for them.

At the end of a long straight I came to a small harbour, the headquarters of Celtic Canal Cruisers, where a cluster of blue and white barges were moored alongside like a queue of water buses. In the distance ahead a church tower and a steeple stood against the sky, a sign that I was approaching the town of Tullamore.

This last stretch into the town was most pleasant. The lock house at the twenty-sixth lock is a period beauty, built by the canal contractor of the time, Michael Hayes, to his own design. It cost £42 more than the standard lock house of the time, but Hayes was proud to provide something special along his stretch of the canal. For a house over 200 years old it is in excellent order, sited in a small garden and fronted by six bright green bushes each trimmed and shaped into a per-

fect globe. Beyond, a line of recently planted poplars lead the tow-path into town past a sign with the town's motto *esto fidelis* which welcomed me to Tullamore. Another sign told me that I had walked 15km from Daingean, and that I was 96km from the river Liffey, presumably where the canal joins it in Ringsend. Tullamore Harbour is a short siding from the main canal; it acted as the terminus of the Grand Canal for a number of years while the directors of the canal argued and schemed about whether or how the line should be continued to the Shannon.

Tullamore, which became the principal town of County Offaly in 1830, is a town of exceptionally fine buildings. The main reasons for the quality of the streets and buildings you see today, apart from the existence near the town of an excellent limestone quarry, are the coming of the canal in 1789, and a strange accident which occurred four years before. In the spring of 1785 the centre of the old town was destroyed in a fire which started when a hot-air balloon became entangled in the chimney of a distillery and set fire to the thatched roof of a cottage.

The first flight of such a balloon had only taken place two years before in 1783, when the brothers Stephen and Joseph Montgolfier of Avignon succeeded in launching a craft using hot air to give it lift. Ireland's first aeronaut was Richard Crosbie, born in Baltinglass in 1750 and described by Jonah Barrington, a contemporary, as 'beyond comparison, the most ingenious mechanic I ever knew'. In August 1784 Crosbie demonstrated his 'Aeronautic Chariot' in Ranelagh Gardens in Dublin, and the following month sent up a balloon carrying a cat which landed in the sea near the Isle of Man. On 9 January 1785, before a crowd of 35,000 people, Crosbie manned one of his own balloons and ascended from Ranalagh Gardens 'with solemn majesty', achieving the first flight in Ireland. After reaching almost two miles in height, he made a descent to Clontarf.

I have not been able find out who was responsible for the Tullamore balloon which caused so much destruction a month or two later, but it could well have been Crosbie, because he had connections with the area through his wife, Charlotte Armstrong, whose family home was in Twickenham, near Ballycumber, about 12km north west of the town.

The disaster of the great fire was turned to advantage by the owner of the town, Charles William Bury. He reached the age of 21 in the same year as the fire and he embarked on an ambitious redevelopment of the town, employing the architect John Pentland in much of the initial planning. The result of the great and swift expansion of trade brought by the Grand Canal and the reconstruction of the town can be seen in the many substantial houses and fine streetscapes that adorn Tullamore today.

The square towered, pinnacled church I had seen from the distance down the canal, which resembled an ancient English cathedral, was St Catherine's Church, designed in 1808 by Francis Johnston, another of the great architects of the day brought in by Charles Bury. In the church is a fine memorial to Charles Moore, the first earl of Charleville, by the sculptor John Van Nost; the monument states 'the late Earl was the last Heir Male of the Moores of Crohan, an Ancient and Honest House'. As he had no 'issue', his nephew, John Bury, inherited his estates, which included 20,000 acres of land around Tullamore. John Bury lived only long enough to commission his uncle's memorial, for he died in a drowning accident in Ringsend only months later. The estate then passed to Charles Bury, an infant at the time. When Bury was created the Earl of Charleville for his development works in Tullamore he commissioned Francis Johnston to design his new home, Charleville Castle. It was completed about 1812, and is probably the finest and most spectacular Gothic Revival castle in Ireland.

Wandering around Tullamore itself, the quality of the late Georgian buildings of the town set a standard which was continued through the nineteenth century into the twentieth century, and the town boasts an excellent collection of fine shopfronts of all periods, including a 1941 example by Michael Scott.

After a wander about I made my way up Colmcille Street to the Bridge House public house, a wonderfully flamboyant building with a façade of brick and elaborate limestone dressings. Inside it was warm, comfortable and a generously spacious place with many different levels and ceiling heights, a conservatory seemingly suspended out over the Tullamore river and a good dining room. It was thronged with people when I arrived and rang with piped country and western music, and a constant stream of people of all ages and descriptions coming and going. I finished my day with an excellent meal in the dining room, after which I walked to the west end of the town, where I had booked bed and breakfast in a house overlooking the canal.

From Tullamore to Banagher,
County Offaly

I awoke the following morning to the splashing sound of heavy rain, and I opened the curtains to see the canal foaming with raindrops and the gutters of the house overflowing. By the look of the puddles it was clear it had been raining all night, and the sky it was down for the day. After a hearty breakfast to build my morale I pulled on my waterproofs and bidding farewell to my landlady, I walked out into the wet, setting out westwards again along the canal. To add to the rain, there was a gusting westerly wind blowing into my face, and as Ferbane was about eighteen miles away, it promised to be an uncomfortable day.

I passed under an ugly modern concrete bridge which was daubed with dull graffiti. A little beyond was a railway bridge with graffiti proclaiming 'Johnny and Liz 1988', clearly painted by a daredevil who had dared to climb out along the girders.

Just after the railway bridge are the ruins of a tower-house overlooking the canal, with some fine cut-stone features and a grand corner machiciolation. Called Shra Castle, it was built about 1588, which makes it a late tower-house, and its creator was John Briscoe, an Elizabethan army officer from Cumberland in England who was granted lands in recognition for his efforts in subduing the Irish in the name of the queen.

I sploshed on through the puddles into the countryside and soon came to Ballycowan Bridge, passing a thatched cottage, the front of which was ablaze with daffodils, brightening up the greyness of the day. Ahead the spectacular towering chimneys of a tall ruin broke the otherwise featureless skyline. It is called Ballycowan Castle, and was built by Thomas Morres in about 1589. At the time the plantation of Offaly was well established, the Irish were subdued, and some English colonisers took the chance to build a new type of house that was more commodious, roomier, and better lit than the early strictly defensive tower-house. A larger plan allowed for a greater number of private rooms, usually separated by timber panelled walls, well-lit by large windows, and heated by many large fireplaces which give this type of building its characteristic, tall and often elaborately decorated chimneys. Ballycowan Castle became the property of Sir Jasper Herbert who extended it, erecting a stone plaque showing his coat of arms, the date 1626 and his family motto, 'By God of might, I hold my right'. An uncompromising colonial, I would think.

Smoke billowed from the chimney of a cottage beside the castle; I noticed that one of its window surrounds matched those in the derelict castle suggesting it was a rarity in Ireland, an occupied seventeenth-century dwelling.

Through the rain ahead a strange silhouette materialised, of two figures poling themselves across the canal on a tiny raft. As I came closer Irish farm labourers, in wellingtons, donkey jackets and caps, could be made out, one holding a

bunch of fenceposts, the other poling a craft that consisted of two planks attached to six polythene drums.

I suppose in the weather conditions we were experiencing nothing would have looked particularly but it seemed that the farms I passed by west of Ballycowan had a neglected look about them. Not every dwelling was run-down; I saw, on the far side of the canal, a long, comfortable-looking bungalow with the name Canal View painted on a sign facing the canal, proclaiming 'Meals and Snacks – Non-Residents welcome'. I trudged on, looking across the water longingly.

The rain came and went in waves, and I walked with head down, seeing little but the immediate surroundings. I was getting very wet and not a little miserable now, splashing, clodding along, the staccato raindrops rattling on the hood of my water-proofs. Every time the rain seemed like easing, it came down again after only a short pause. Eventually the rain came through my Gortex hood, and I had to put on my woolly hat which I had been husbanding dry in my rucksack for later on, because I still had a long way to go. My arms and knees were beginning to feel damp and cold where Irish rain was penetrating the miracle Gortex, but, on the bright side, my feet were still warm and dry. Time seemed to telescope as I trudged along, and I was surprised to be awoken from my reveries to find that I had reached Corcoran's Bridge, near the village of Rahan.

The rain had eased off, but if the weather had been better I would have had a bit of a celebration here, because Rahan marked roughly the halfway point of my journey across Ireland. I had come about 98 miles from the sea at Dalkey to the rain at Rahan, and it quite cheered me up. I was not far away, about twenty miles, from the traditionally accepted 'centre' of all Ireland, a pillar-stone erected in 1769 near the village of Glasson in Westmeath. I was boosted by the thought of my progress, and decided to take time out to have a look at the monastic site at Rahan, a short distance to the north. I turned onto a road leading away from the canal, and crossed a field towards what remained of the monastic settlement, including a surviving roofed church standing in a stone-walled enclosure surrounded by a cemetery of Celtic crosses. The only clues that tell this is something special were the east window and doorway, but I had read that under the slated roof erected in the eighteenth century is an ancient barrel-vault, and that the internal details suggest Byzantine influences. Unfortunately the place was locked and I was not able to see these. I had to be satisfied, however, with the beautiful Romanesque east doorway, and above it a unique circular window, made of sandstone decoratively carved in exquisite detail.

I left part of my over-trousers on a barbed-wire fence climbing out into the field again, where a roofless ruin of another church, this one built in the twelfth century, stood bleak and solitary in a desert of well-cropped nitrogen-fed grass. It had a fine, chevron-decorated Romanesque doorway which had unfortunately lost its flanking columns, and the eastern gable was decorated with the head of a bishop carved in the window moulding. I found fragments of a third church in the graveyard, where I was aurally assaulted by a family of wrens; the cock perched on top of a tombstone and rattled and clicked at me with great vehemence, while the rest added their voices, flitting in and out of the undergrowth. I was surprised to find gravestones with Crucifixion scenes carved on them, one with a hammer, pliers and nails dated 1791 with the sun and moon also featuring. It was an eerie graveyard, with tombstones at all angles, ash trees bursting forth from graves, and an old yew tree hung down with a shroud of ivy.

The surviving pre-Norman church here at Rahan, where St Cartach founded a monastery in AD 580, still roofed and in use, is a rarity in Ireland.

James Molloy was baptised here in 1837. Although his name is not well-remembered, his work certainly is: he wrote the words and music of such works as 'The Kerry Dancers', 'Darby and Joan', and that romantic and melodious song that for some reason always reminds me of my fraternal grandmother, 'Love's Old Sweet Song'. Song-writing was not his chosen career; he studied law in Dublin and London and was called to the Bar in 1872, but his music must have taken over, because he never practised law.

Time was marching on, however, and although I would have liked to explore a little more, I returned to the canal tow-path and continued towards Ferbane. As the canal reached westwards into open countryside, was a great extent of raised bogs to the south while to the north there was a bare, green landscape with just a wooded hill in the distance to relieve the flatness. I knew the river Clodiagh, tributary to the Brosna, was nearby now, and could see the green grassy mounds of material that had been dredged out of the river and left on the bank during drainage works a number of years ago.

The slight lull in the rain had brought the birds out to fill the air again with birdsong. I spotted a pair of snipe only a few metres ahead of me; they made a diving, dodging escape over the canal-side hedge. A moment later I stopped trans-fixed as an otter, shiny black, came out of the undergrowth and in one continuous liquid movement flowed across the tow-path, sliding into the reed-fringed canal without as much

as a ripple. I watched quietly to see if he would surface, but saw nothing. As I walked on, however, there was a commotion in a thick reedbed on the far side and a pair of mallards came splashing and squawking out of it, slapping the surface of the water with their feet as they made emergency take-offs and flew together downstream. Of the otter, which no doubt caused the panic, there was no sign.

Beyond Rahan at Ballincloghan and Cornalaur the countryside had quite a prosperous look to it, and there was a good scatter of modern well-built bungalows and sturdy nineteenth-century farmhouses. Displayed on the front lawn of one of the modern houses, was an old ploughshare, a mangle and a crane from an open cottage fireplace, with a fine array of cast iron pots hanging from it, now filled with daffodils after a lifetime of soup and spuds.

After Cornalaur Bridge I entered another extensive field of bleak bogland, and the rain came down again. There was no shelter now from the gale and rain coming directly across the flatlands to the west, with only a few stands of thin birch to soften the blow. I felt like a sailing boat tacking against the wind, hunched over trying to make my outline as small as possible.

There was no sign of life in any of the cottages I passed, no warm glow in a window, and I kept looking for a friendly face peering out who would see me, have pity, and ask me in for a cup of tea in front of a roaring fire. But there was no turf smoke coming from any chimney.

At the end of a very long straight some trees and the silhouette of a church tower against the western sky came into view, signalling that Pollagh was not much farther on. This hamlet, a settlement which dates from the establishment of the peat industry on the Turraun bog to the west and south in the 1850s, was referred to by Todd Andrews, appointed by Seán Lemass in 1933 to oversee the development of Ireland's bogs, as having 'evident squalor and poverty on a scale much worse than I had ever seen in the Dublin slums of my youth ... it was truly the home of the Bog-Man tradition'.

When I eventually reached the pub I was devastated to find that no food other than crisps and peanuts was on offer. Faced with such disappointment, and with no inclination to return to the tow-path immediately, I consoled myself with a hot whiskey, which smoothly ran into another and then a third before I felt like donning the wet gear again. When I left the pub it was still raining, but the previously grey world had taken on a golden glow, which remained with me for a number of miles towards Ferbane.

I crossed the high bridge at Pollagh over to the north bank to visit the church; I had been very impressed by the altar furniture on my last visit, and I wanted to see if my enthusiasm had been encouraged by John Jameson, blender and purveyor of fine whiskeys. It was a neat building with gothic windows and a plaque on the wall stating it was built by the faithful of the locality in 1907. It had an unusual fan-shaped plan, with the altar flanked by a polychrome pair of Harry Clarke windows as the focal point. The altar was fashioned from the rich, dark brown, Medusa-like tangle of roots and trunks of bog yew, and the tabernacle was encased in a similar chaotic matrix of polished roots. The sculptor who had tamed these natural forms was Michael Casey of Lemanaghan, a few miles to the north west, who has become well known in recent years for his work with bog timbers; a plaque said that the wood used for the altar and tabernacle was 4,800 years old. Michael Casey's work was even more impressive on my second visit.

While I was admiring the work a man came in to say a prayer, something which used to be common in churches all over Ireland, but has now almost entirely died out because churches cannot safely be left open and unattended. When he was finished and had made a vague hand movement representing the sign of the cross, he sidled up to me. He was a tall man in his sixties wearing an old gaberdine coat and a tweed cap, both darkened with rain.

'D'ye like it?' he asked.

I told him I thought it was strangely beautiful and asked him what the congregation thought about it.

'Oh, it's highly thought of,' he said, 'and it's wood that came out of the bog, in the same way as the bricks which built the church. You see, the people around Pollagh,' he pronounced 'poll' with a 'gull' sound, 'used to make bricks for building and sell them to builders in Tullamore and places. Under the bog, when the peat is taken off, there's great patches of brick clay, and they used to put it into brick moulds and fire them in little kilns. Each brickmaker in the parish contributed 100 bricks towards the church. Although they don't make them any more, they're sought after, and you'd have to pay more than a pound each for salvaged ones.'

The brick industry began as a cottage industry in the late eighteenth century, but with the coming of the canal, it became possible to ship large quantities of bricks, and for a period of about 60 years large quantities were exported to Dublin and other centres; in the 1840s about 4,000 tons of bricks were sent east by canal from the brickworks between Pollagh and Tullamore. With the influx of cheaper bricks from Britain, and the mechanisation of brick-making in Dublin some years later, the industry reverted to its cottage status, and had continued as such up to recent years.

He was taken aback when I told him I was walking from Tullamore to Ferbane. 'God, you're a hardy man', he crowed. 'As hardy as the men who built the canal. They were a great race, and they had great foresight.

'D'you know, at each lock when they constructed it, they planted a copse of oak trees so that the material would be on hand to replace the locks after 70 years. Have a look as you go along, there's still some of those trees left.'

He had great knowledge about the building of the canal and talked as if it had only been completed the week before.

'Look out for them trees,' he said as we parted outside the church, and I crossed the bridge again, continuing westwards into the wind.

The landscape around was desolate, dark bog scattered with birch scrub; the man I had met in the church had told me that an acre of land out here is more valuable than an acre in County Meath, but it was hard to believe. Nearby, to the north, I could see glimpses of silver as the river Brosna, joined somewhere north of Pollagh by the Clodiagh, meandered near the canal. In the early stages of planning the Grand Canal, Thomas Omer had planned to save money by using the Brosna for the last stretch into the Shannon, but it proved inpracticable. In fact to keep the two watercourses apart, the canal has to loop south of Ferbane instead of heading straight and economically on through Ferbane.

Otter spraints or droppings were becoming quite common along the canal bank, in some of which the rain had exposed the tiny white bones of fish and small mammals. There were also areas of tossed and flattened grass that hinted at the frequent presence of otters. In a country which lacks the rich variety of species our neighbours enjoy, it is nice to know that we at least have the densest population of otters

in western Europe, having somehow avoided the rapid population loss experienced elsewhere. Spraints have even been
found under O'Connell Bridge in the centre of Dublin city.
The otter is regarded as vulnerable on a world-wide scale,
which makes the Irish population, and the need to conserve
it, of international importance.

A couple of miles beyond Pollagh I followed the canal
over the Boora river which drains the bogland south of the
canal into the Brosna. Bogs hide and preserve the past, and
during the cutting of Irish bogs for fuel much has been
revealed about the people and the landscape of prehistory;
the Boora area is no exception. It was once one of the largest
raised bogs in the midlands, but it has now been almost completely cut away, and a tiny lake it contained, Lough Boora,
was drained in the 1950s. Beneath the bog a long line of
stones was exposed which was thought at first to have been
an ancient causeway. Later examination, however, showed
that the stones had been the storm beach of an earlier, far
larger Lough Boora, which had existed here after the Ice Age,
before the bog began to form. Along this fossilised shoreline
archaeologists found abundant evidence of the presence of
the earliest colonisers of Ireland, Mesolithic people who
camped here 9,000 years ago. The remains of the hearths of
their settlement fires and examples of their tools and their
weapons have been found. Modern, painstaking archaeological methods have even revealed the remains of the meals
these, our earliest ancestors, ate. Besides fish, berries and
fruits, their menu included red deer, wild pigs, hares and birds
including whooper swans, which still, 9,000 years later, fly
south from northern Russia to winter here every year. Under
the microscope fossilised spores found on what had been the
lake bottom created a picture of the landscape these people

lived in, a wilderness of forests of oaks, elms and hazels, rich in wild fowl and fish lining the shores of the great lake.

By the time I reached Derry Bridge the rain and wind were really taking their toll, and I trudged on, feeling real tiredness now, and finding it a considerable effort to push against the wind. Even the sight of a hare slowly crossing a few metres in front of me failed to excite much interest, nor did the predominance of the name 'Derry' in this locality on my rain-soaked map, which in good conditions would have had me considering how far back the name was coined, when the last remnants of oak forests clung to little patches of higher ground as the bog flowed over all else.

Two hours after leaving Pollagh I reached McCartney's Aqueduct, named after Sir James McCartney, a chairman of the Grand Canal Company who was knighted at the Ringsend docks during the canal opening ceremony. It takes the canal over the Silver River, close to which the Ferbane power station stands. The canal continues along on top of a rampart across the bog, a cross-country promenade that would make a great walk in summertime. The embankment took 3,000 men to complete, and the difficulties involved are evidenced in the fact that in all, 22 contractors were involved in the eight-mile stretch of canal across the bog here. It is said that many of the problems were caused by local people deliberately creating breaches in the embankment in order to get work.

As I passed a cottage that had been partially demolished, I noted the bricks had been carefully stacked, and remembered what the man in Pollagh had said about their value. Soon after, to my great relief, I reached the bridge carrying the road north to Ferbane, now less than 1km away. I had little interest, I am afraid, in Gallen Priory which I passed on the way, and before long I reached the town and made my way into Heiny's pub. It occupies the site of a very old inn called The Black Boot, which was owned in the mid-eighteenth century by Patrick Coughlan, a descendant of the MacCoughlan clan who held lordship over a broad area of lands between here and the Shannon since medieval times. Although the family were Catholic, in common with many Irish families, Patrick's line made the change in the late seventeenth century, as is evidenced by the following notice in the local news-sheet for 12 July 1755:

> The Independent Electors of King's Co., who met at Ballycumber on the 1st July to celebrate the happy event of the Battle of the Boyne, have adjourned, and will meet again, at the house of Patrick Coughlan, on the 1st August.

I stripped off my waterproofs which had turned out to be anything but, and reckoned that the expensive breathable Gortex must have choked to death or drowned some time earlier.

There were a few men perched on bar stools at the bar, silently watching the television and nursing pints. I knew I had arrived in heaven when the girl behind the bar told me they could do a steak for me with all the 'trimmings'. While I was waiting I had a pint of Guinness, and was on my second by the time the steak arrived. After an hour or two, fed, warmed up and feeling quite drowsy, I dragged on my wet gear once again and went up town to check into my Bed and Breakfast. By 9.30pm I was in bed and asleep.

The following day dawned calm, sunny and warm, the air full of birdsong, and well provisioned with sausages, rashers and eggs washed down with tea, I set out for Banagher just after 9am. What a glorious day it was, and such a contrast from the day before – it was typical of the Irish weather; nothing, good or bad, ever lasts for long. I had on a previous occasion attempted to follow an angler's path along the bank of the Brosna river, which flows through Ferbane, to Shannon Harbour; some locals had told me that it was the best way to go. Because of high water levels, however, I found the path was impassable a short distance from the town, and had to return to the canal. I was going to follow the canal as before, but I would look out for the dismantled railway line between Ferbane and Banagher to see if any of it could be followed.

Ferbane is located on a low hill overlooking the canal, but even a low hill is a vantage point in these low-lying parts, and in the clarity of the clear air left by the rain I could see southwards for many miles. I took a side road towards the canal and soon came upon two tinker's caravans and a large trailer, like a goods container, that was fitted out as a mobile workshop, tucked in by the hedge. In the workshop two young men were working on what looked like a diesel generator. A neatly-dressed, blond-haired child with bright eyes and rosy cheeks ran up to me and said 'Hello!' She was followed by two other children, a boy and a girl, and they all gazed up with big smiles as if I was an expected guest. I returned their greetings and asked them their names. As they were breathlessly telling me, all together, one of the young men came down out of the workshop and apologised if they were bothering me.

He was a strong-looking lad with a great head of curly hair and sparkling white teeth. I wished him a good morning and he said they had been up since dawn servicing the generator, it was a rush job. I said it was a grand sheltered spot they had, and he replied they had been there a couple of weeks but had a job coming up in Kilcormac and would be moving off as soon as they were finished. I spotted a small cage beside one of the caravans and asked what they had caught.

'Oh we didn't catch it, we got it from a man in Banagher,' the young man said, and brought me over to see, opening the cage.

A sleek and bright-eyed ferret looked out at me, the first time I can remember seeing one 'live'.

'He won't come out,' the man said.

The children gathered around the cage calling him, 'Paddy, Paddy come on!'

A striking-looking woman in her late twenties came out of one of the caravans to join in the fun.

Paddy stayed put, however, sniffing the air and eyeing us all suspiciously.

'What do you do with him?' I asked.

'Oh we use him rabbiting. He ketches the rabbits for us, he's a great rabbiter. We put him down the hole, and block it. We'd have a line on him so he wouldn't run away. He did though wance and was gone for three weeks, but he came back again.'

'I suppose because he's so well looked after – look at his shiny coat,' I commented. 'Isn't he very like a stoat, but much bigger.'

'More like a mink, I'd say,' he replied.

I asked him what the animal ate.

'Fish and bread, mainly.'

We chatted on a while longer, and then I waved goodbye and continued on my way. These were real 'tinkers', and I use the name not as a derogatory term, but as a proud and descriptive name for the industrious, well-liked people I remember from my childhood who roamed the rural areas of Ireland and were skilled in the art of repairing or making tin artefacts, an early service industry. They were young, blooming with health, and clearly, as their ancestors did before them, were performing a useful service to society. These were real country folk, practising old traditional customs.

I disturbed two pheasants in the grassy verge as I proceeded along the road, a cock and a hen, and characteristically they ran rather than flew away, and swiftly veered out of sight into a field of long grass.

Reaching the canal I turned westwards again to follow it, walking along a comfortable, meandering tow-path on the north bank. I was surprised by the change in the weather, and how wonderfully pleasant the surroundings were in the morning sun. The canal reflected a blue sky, disturbed only by the fish taking leaps out of the water, the far bank lined with daffodils, and the songs of wrens and robins following me from the hedges. The reeds along the canal edge here had been carefully harvested, for thatching I guessed. A heron lazily took off before me and with slow wingbeats moved on to a stand further on. I was surprised by a jet black cormorant with a bright orange beak flying briskly along the canal heading east; one is not used to seeing cormorants inland and I wondered was he from the western seaboard or the Shannon, and where he was heading for.

The water in the canal was very low, and there was a not unpleasant fishy smell. The Brosna came very close now to the canal and at one stage, as it passed an old ruined mill building flanked by ivy-covered oaks, only a pair of cows were wanting to make it a perfect Constable scene. The Brosna was also at a lower level, and was flowing fast compared to the canal. At the point where it came closest to the canal, a mere 100m or so, I came across the remains of a bridge which once took the old railway over the canal, but the line was completely overgrown and inaccessible.

At Judge's Bridge I found that a road which crossed the canal vanished through disuse on the north side; its ghost, still lined with hedgerows, led to a tall and gaunt ivy-clad ruin that locals told me was called Judge's House. The Judge in this case is a name rather than a profession; before it belonged to the Judge family, this house was owned by the Sheils, from whom the townsland here, Ballysheil, got its name. The O'Sheils were hereditary physicians to the MacCoughlan clan who ruled over the area in the Middle Ages.

A short distance on I came to the harbour of Belmont, a pretty milling village established in the eighteenth century on the Brosna river. A considerable collection of mill buildings and warehouses survive, and north of the canal is a fine weir on the Brosna. At the canal harbour the lock-keeper told me that because of the considerable rainfall the previous day the canal locks had to be opened to prevent flooding, which explained the low water levels I had seen.

Along the grassy harbour edge I came across a dozen English anglers, all with their stools, boxes of lures and flies and buckets of squirming, bright-coloured mealworms. They all sat a few yards apart, staring as if mesmerised into the calm waters of the canal where the almost invisible lines from their rods entered the water. One of them told me they were from Manchester, and came regularly in two mini-buses for the fishing and the craic in Ireland.

My map suggested that the old railway crossed again between Cloghan and Clonony but I saw nothing resembling

it. The Clara to Banagher line was known as the 'Midland Counties and Shannon Junction Railway Company' when it opened in 1884, and it linked up the Dublin to Clara line with the Shannon steamers at Banagher, which would take passengers south as far as Killaloe from where you could reach Limerick. Like so many small railways around the country, the line was closed by Todd Andrews in 1963.

At Clonony Bridge I took a ten minute detour to see the remains of Clonony Castle. The ruin, reached through an arched gateway, is impressive, built as it is on a rocky promontory with a substantial amount of the bawn walls surviving.

I asked an old fellow passing along the road did he know anything about the place.

'Aw, if I learned all these things when I was young I'd know them now, but I didn't bother when I was young and I, ah sure, I've no interest now. Like you know, I wouldn't be able to learn all those things now, but there was people here one time in Clonony who knew all these things but they're gone now.' And then, as an afterthought he added, 'Oh, Ann Boleyn's sister is buried under the bush there.'

He went on to tell me that the castle had not been inhabited for over 100 years but that he used to go to dances in it up to the last war, until the local Parish Priest, afraid that someone would have an accident on the battlements, or more probably concerned that immoral activities might be going on upstairs, had the stairs broken down, as Cromwell had done to so many Irish tower-houses to make them uninhabitable. The local man's Boleyn story arises from the existence of a grave slab in the grounds of the castle, which bears the almost eroded inscription:

Hereunder leys Elizabeth and Mary Bullyn daughter of
Thomas Bullyn son of George Bullyn the son of George
Bullyn Viscount Rochford son of Thomas Bullyn Erle of
Ormond and Willsheer

The inscription suggests that the two women were
cousins of the unfortunate Anne Boleyn, probably refugees
from the wrath of Henry VIII after their cousin had been executed, but in my researches I could not find any account of
how they came to be in this Offaly outpost of the
MacCoughlans.

I rejoined the canal and continued a little more than 1km
to reach the decayed canal village of Shannon Harbour. The
place is very dilapidated, the old hotel roofless and suffocat-
ed with ivy; the canal lined with pleasure craft of all kinds in
hibernation, many of them the jalopies of the waterways.
There was nothing here on the Shannon banks before the
canal came, but the village which grew up subsequently must
have known exciting times in the heyday of canal travel and
transport in the early 1800s.

Although work had commenced on the Grand Canal in
1757, it was 1804 before the first trade boat to travel from
Dublin entered the Shannon from the canal; the crew were
each presented with a new suit of clothes to mark the occasion. The Grand Canal project had cost around £877,000, a
lot of money in those days, one-quarter coming from public
funds and the rest from private sources. By 1810 nearly
20,000 tons of cargo were being transported annually on the
canal but the capital cost of the construction works and the
ongoing maintenance meant that it could only keep going
with the aid of further government grants. The improvements
in roads and the technology of horse-drawn coaches, togeth-

er with the emergence of the railways, sounded an early death-knell, but the canal struggled on as a transport system until the last commercial traffic passed through in 1960. The possibility that the waterways would be closed permanently was campaigned against by an initially small but determined group of leisure users, who proved the amenity importance of the canal by organising the first Shannon Boat Rally in 1961, attracting 70 leisure craft. In 1963 the Irish Tourist Board spent £140,000 on the improvement of facilities which led to the waterways becoming a significant new tourism product. After a brief period of decline, during which Dublin Corporation came near to filling it in and covering it with an urban motorway around the south suburbs, the canal was transferred from CIE ownership to the Office of Public Works and its future was assured.

I walked westwards a further 2km to reach the spot where the canal entered the Shannon, and looked across the broad silver waterway to get my first glimpse of the province of Connaught and County Galway.

At 344km from its source to the sea, the Shannon is the longest river in the British Isles, and it drains a catchment area of over 15,000 square km or one-fifth of the land mass of the island of Ireland. It is more, however, than just a river to Ireland and the Irish; it had and has a major influence on the landscape of the island, an influence that has insured its significant contribution to the history of the land and its peoples from the earliest times. It is said to have been named after Sinann, daughter of Lodan and niece of Manannan, after whom the Isle of Man is named. Lodan and Manannan were leaders of the Tuatha de Danann, early semi-mythical inhabitants of Ireland. She is said to have drowned at the river's birth, attempting to harvest magical fruits which grew around the legendary Connla's Well, an activity which was reserved in those non-politically correct times for male warriors.

When the glaciers retreated from the Irish mainland 12,000 years ago one of the main features of the ice-carved island they it left behind was an extensive central lowland area of lakes and rivers that all but divided the land mass in two along the line the Shannon now follows. Within a few centuries the bare but rich-clayed landscape was colonised by trees, shrubs and herbs, resulting in a thickly wooded country laced through with a matrix of swamps, rivers and lakes, much like areas of the Amazon basin are today. When the earliest human colonisers arrived in Ireland, probably in the northern part of the island more than 9,000 years ago, cross-country travel by land would have been all but impossible, and they used the network of waterways, in particular the Shannon 'sea', to travel south seeking good fishing and hunting. Later the great waterway was used for trade as the Stone Age gave way to the Bronze Age which in turn gave way to the Iron Age. In the National Museum in Dublin there is a 20metre long dug-out canoe which was found in a bog in east Galway some years ago; it is typical of the craft used in some numbers in the Shannon basin 2,500 years ago. As the great forests were cut down and cleared over succeeding centuries and the valuable alluvial soils along the water's edge were gradually reclaimed for farming, the Shannon river as we know it today came into being, connecting Lough Ree and Lough Derg, ancestors of the old inland sea.

I left Shannon Harbour and, turning south for a change, walked down the road towards Banagher, for the first time in over 100km not following a canal. The Shannon was in spring flood and to my right it broadened out until it lapped the low roadside ditch and spread itself far into the fields to our left. For a few hundred metres the road became a cause-way raised only a foot or so above the water level. In winter the road here is sometimes completely inundated as the Shannon's waters spread out, and families of swans, mute and whooper, sail majestically across.

The area is the southern part of the Shannon Callows where extensive tracts of meadowland are inundated when the river bursts its banks every winter. It is not until early the following summer that the land has dried out sufficiently for the rich grasses it leaves behind to be mowed. There are no houses or roads, and few trees in this riverine corridor of 3,500 hectares extent which straddles the Shannon between Shannonbridge and Portumna, and it is an important habitat for flora and fauna. The delay in cutting hay necessitated by the damp conditions is one of the factors which has ensured a tenuous survival of the rare corncrake in the callows. This shy bird was once common all over Ireland; indeed, country folk from all parts of the country who are over 50 remember its call but it almost became extinct when annually killed in large numbers during the cutting of early grass. In the cal-lows, however, it has time to rear its young and lead them away before the harvesting begins. It is, however, a bird which has not been capable of adapting to the changes in agricultural practices that threaten its existence, and from my brief experience, seems to have a poor sense of danger.

A background of curlew's calls punctuated by the sharp-er piping of oystercatchers gave an eerie atmosphere to the beautiful surroundings as I walked. Lines of fence posts, each a perch for a redshank, stretched across the waters aimlessly, and clumps of trees in the distance rose like islands from the calm water. Numerous tight formations of waders skimmed across the glass-like surface, and far out, a long way away, I

could see shelducks and other wildfowl in great numbers. A hump-backed bridge on the road indicated that I had again connected with the Clara to Banagher railway, a barely discernable narrow band of sheep-cropped grass emerging from scrub to the north east, running under the bridge and disappearing into a hazel jungle that lined the flooded Shannon to the south west. On the previous occasion I had walked here, I had attempted to follow it towards the river and, I hoped, Banagher, but abruptly I had come to a place where there had been a collapse, across which a torrent of water flowed. The causeway continued to the mainland some distance away, but it was too broad to safely jump, and the force of the water and its unknown depth made me unwilling to try to wade, so once again I had to turn back to the road.

So this time I continued, reluctantly, along the road into Banagher, choosing to enter the town by a side road which took me up onto a broad hill, from where the views were wonderful. Behind I could, with binoculars, see the cooling towers at Ferbane and identify Clonony Castle. Northwards the Shannon basin stretched towards a hilly horizon, a mass of apparent lakes and islands. The road seemed to go on forever through Banagher's outskirts before I reached the town proper. I went into William Lyons' Bar for refreshments, an emporium wherein you can buy a wide range of things from Texaco petrol to angling gear, from guns and ammunition to alcohol, and if you have any wool, the proprietor might buy it from you.

Here I met some of the English anglers I had come across some hours earlier at Belmont; in the meantime they had had time to finish up fishing and come here to get quite drunk. One of them, a little more sober than the rest, told me that a few of them were officially on the dole in England, and did not want to be seen on holiday, so Ireland was a good place to come. I found that William Lyons, in spite of the wide range of things he sold, did not have sandwiches, but he told me I would be well-fed in Commercial House, so I left after one beer, and made my way through the town.

Outside the library I stopped to examine two great blocks of limestone lying on the roadside, one inscribed 'County of Galway' and the other 'Kings County'. A passer by told me they were from the old bridge which was demolished in the 1840s. Commercial House was in the main street, run by two broad bellied, smiling, busy men who could have been brothers, in immaculate sparkling white shirts. It was a comfortable and welcoming place, and I was well looked after with a full 'plate o' mate' lunch.

Banagher is a bustling town with a rich and interesting heritage which its citizens are just beginning to recognise. Sir William Wilde, antiquarian and writer, and father of Oscar, went to boarding school here, as did William Bulfin, author of *Rambles in Éireann,* a wonderful description of late nineteenth-century Ireland viewed from the saddle of a bike. The school was housed in Cuba Court, an eighteenth-century mansion that was described by Maurice Craig as the most masculine house in Ireland; the building was bulldozed only a few years ago. Charlotte Brontë spent her honeymoon here after marrying the local rector, though she died some months later.

Anthony Trollope, who was based in Banagher as a Post Office surveyor commenced his first novel, *The MacDermots of Ballycloran,* here. I went up the main street to where someone said his house was, and, spotting one recently renovated but with a traditional character, I knocked on the door to ask permission to take a photograph. An elderly woman

answered, and when she saw the camera, pulled back shyly as she thought I wanted to take a picture of her. She did not know about Trollope, but thought maybe he lived next door. Next door was a disappointingly modern house with no apparent characteristics of the nineteenth century, so I went on my way. I afterwards found that the modern-looking house was indeed the one Trollope had lived in.

I found the tourist office housed in Crank House, a wonderful, bow-fronted eighteenth-century building with a Gibbsian doorcase, that is, made up of chunky blocks of stone. There is another house just like it in Tullamore's Cormac Street, called The Round House. The mail staff in the tourist office had never heard of Cuba Court, the ruins of which I wanted to see, but after much discussion, they called the manager who said it was deeply disappointing and a great loss for the people of Banagher that the house has been demolished, and there was little point in seeking out the ruins as there was not a wall standing.

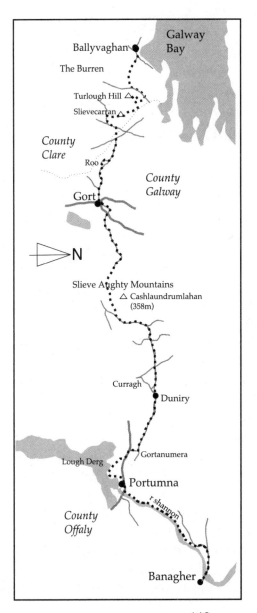

PART THREE

SUMMER:
Banagher
to
Ballyvaghan

From Banagher to Portumna,
County Galway

It was early summer before I could arrange to get away from Dublin again to complete the final stage of my journey from the Irish Sea to the Atlantic. The last leg of my walk from Banagher to Ballyvaghan was about 85km, which I had divided into five stages, the first of which was from Banagher to the town of Portumna, about 19 kilometres away at the northern tip of Lough Derg.

I set off down the main street towards the bridge over the Shannon a little before 9am. I practically skipped across the river into the county of Galway and the province of Connaught, getting maybe a tiny sense of the freedom that keeps travellers, tramps and tinkers on the move. Upstream of the bridge, lines of Shannon cruisers lay moored to jetties, while downstream the river narrowed and was overlooked from both banks by ivy-covered military buildings of various periods; this has been a strategically important crossing place since the first bridge is said to have been built here in 1049 by Roderic O'Connor, King of Connaught.

While the Shannon has always been an important route

for north-south communication, it has also served as a considerable barrier to east-west progress. Travel from Dublin to Galway in a reasonably direct line involves having to cross the river some place along the 35-mile stretch between Lough Derg and Lough Ree. The few fording places and bridges that existed along this stretch were strategically very important, and more than once the Shannon formed the 'front line' between opposing forces, as it did towards the end of the Williamite wars when the Jacobites held the land west of the river and constructed defensive works at strategic points between Athlone and Portumna.

The present bridge was completed in 1843, and at its western end stands a Martello tower and the reconstructed stump of a McCoughlan tower-house. These fortifications are part of an impressive line of defences designed to deny back-door access through the Shannon river to the hinterland of Ireland.

During my preparatory research into a walking route across Ireland I had made some enquiries about the possibility of walking along the banks of the Shannon to Portumna but was unable to ascertain if it were possible or not. I eventually decided that I would have to follow the narrow public roads which wound southwards west of the river and subsequently I followed this route on foot. A short time after I had completed my first reconnaissance for the route to Ballyvaghan, the historian Canon Egan, with whom I had corresponded about the historical buildings of the area west of Portumna, suggested that there seemed to be an embankment along the river that might be walkable, although he was aware that some sections might be impassable with brambles and overgrowth. The embankment had been built during the late 1920s as part of the Ardnacrusha hydro-electric power station works, and was in the care of the ESB. On a further reconnaissance trip I located this embankment and found it was indeed viable. It has since, I understand, become part of a major Greenway walking route from Bantry to Leitrim. My route for the day, therefore, would take me west of the Shannon for a few kilometres before I would loop around and follow this great embankment all the way to the bridge that spanned the river at Portumna.

The Shannon soon disappeared behind as I followed the main road for a couple of uneventful miles into County Galway, and then turned south onto a side road at Rooaun. The single lane side road meandered out onto open flatlands that aeons ago must have been beneath the surface of a broader Shannon, and as the trees became scarce the great dome of the mottled cloudy sky became the major feature of the scene. At a rambling farmhouse, where the air was filled with a cacophony of turkeys, geese and hens competing with the hedgerow birds for the loudest and longest tirade, I reached the shore of the Shannon again at Keelogue, since ancient times a fording place of the river. For some distance below Banagher the course of the Shannon is split by a series of islands, and across the stream I could see one of them, Incherky, and between the trees that overgrow it, the squat, ivy-covered Keelogue Battery, another Napoleonic Wars relic. Near here, when excavations were being carried out to deepen the river in the1840s, ancient artefacts representing previous eras were dredged up from the bed of the river, including stone axeheads, bronze swords and the remains of early firearms; is it not odd that the weapons of war seem to last longer than most other more worthwhile things?

I now took care to look out for some access to the river bank, and it did not take long to spot what seemed to be a suitable stile crossing the hedge in the right direction.

I had not enquired whether or not one was allowed to walk on the embankment but there was no sign at the stile warning me off. A few hundred mucky metres beyond the stile, past a great rushing weir, the path led out onto a grassy 2m-wide embankment. The top was only a metre above swampy ground on the river side, but double that above the land on the right. The place was teeming with birds. Grey wagtails, thrushes, chaffinches and wrens sang and sported about the thick reed and willow margins of the river, beyond which a pair of cormorants took off ponderously from the water on my arrival, their black silhouettes startling against the bright sky.

As I strode down the embankment with the broad river flowing smoothly to my left, the grey bulk of Meelick church appeared ahead. There has been a church at this place since ancient times, when, before the advent of bridges, Meelick was, with Keelogue, one of the few fording points of the lower Shannon. The present church with its great east window, a masterpiece of swirling stone tracery, is of medieval date, and has been continuously in use for at least 500 years. It is surrounded by the ruins of a more extensive complex of stone buildings and earthen banks, what remains of the original abbey complex. On my previous visit I had taken a look at the interior, and found it a quiet place, even in contrast with the external peaceful surroundings.

A castle was erected to guard the ford here at the extreme western bounds of Norman influence by William de Burgo in 1203, and the continuing importance of the place is signified by the battles and skirmishes that took place nearby in subsequent centuries. The castle was levelled and burned on a number of occasions, the last being during the reign of

Elizabeth I. During the Napoleonic Wars a barracks was established here as part of the fortifications which can be seen on an island in the river, but today Meelick village is a lonely place, a row of deserted houses and a tiny shop over-looking an empty street, all probably built from the stones of the former castles, barracks and Friary.

In the winter of 1602 it is thought that O'Sullivan Beare's clan crossed the Shannon somewhere south of here. Under sporadic attack along the east bank by the loyalist MacEgans, once proud custodians of the Brehon law in Ireland, they had to improvise curraghs made from the skins of their slaughtered animals to cross the river. O'Sullivan Beare thought it would be friendlier on the western side but they were immediately attacked there by the O'Maddens from nearby Derryhiveney, and they had to leave their dead behind as they made their escape towards Aughrim.

Leaving Meelick behind, I followed the embankment southwards. To the east I could see a long low range of hills which I took to be the Slieve Blooms but otherwise all was so flat that one could see nothing beyond the overgrown islands in the middle of the river, from one of which rose another Martello tower. Little groups of lambs huddled together below the embankment, their mothers all in a bunch 100 yards away, heads down busily feeding. These, I presumed, were the reason why the grass surface on the embankment was shorn to the smoothness of a billiard table, providing the most comfortable walking surface I had experienced since starting my journey at Dalkey.

A little farther on I came to a shed which I believe hous-es one of the many pumps needed along this stretch to pump tributaries up into the Shannon, which the embankment kept at an artificially higher level than the land around. The

Shannon, for all its length, is a remarkably 'flat' river, the only significant fall occurring on the 24km stretch between Killaloe and Limerick. It was the potential of this slight fall that inspired Thomas McLaughlin, engineer and mathematician, to propose in 1923 a hydro-electric scheme on the Shannon to provide electric power on a nationwide basis, a great new and modern venture for the infant state. The proposal, involving the construction of a power station at Ardnacrusha, below Killaloe, was guided through to the Cabinet table in 1924 by Patrick McGilligan, Minister for Industry and Commerce, and became a live project when a contract was signed with Siemens-Schukert for the construction works in 1925. It is difficult today to comprehend what a gigantic engineering feat the construction of this project involved. Apart from the engineering works necessary, there were a number of serious difficulties to be overcome. For instance, the site was without adequate roads or a railway, yet all the machinery used had to be imported and the cranes on the Limerick docks were not big enough to unload the heavy turbine hardware being imported from Germany, In addition, there was nowhere to house the thousands of workers that would be required. All these matters were, however, efficiently and speedily dealt with, and work began in September 1925.

An old man in a pub in Banagher who had worked on the project told me the money was great. Conditions on the site were primitive, however, and many of the navvies, who had come from all over Ireland, worked 70 hours a week. One contingent of Connemara men who walked south from their homes to Limerick because they did not have the bus fare, spoke only Irish, and owned only one báinín suit each. He remembered with some amazement at this remove that some

of them waded into the Shannon fully clothed, even in the depths of winter, to wash the dirt and grime from their clothes. The money gave a lot of west of Ireland men a taste for the high life, so many left for England at the end of the project and spent the rest of their lives working on major construction projects there.

Four years after work started, the first electric current from the Shannon was fed into the national system. In January 1930, when the Pigeonhouse coal-burning station in Dublin was taken out of service, Ardnacrusha became the sole generating station serving the whole country. Today the station produces only three per cent of the country's needs.

Eventually, having passed south of the islands in the middle of the river, I saw the far bank for the first time. The calls of curlews echoed around me for most of the way, and swans were quite common, but of herons I only saw two between Banagher and Portumna, one spiralling like an eagle high in the sky, something I have only seen once before. The surface was wonderful, the weather good, and my only concern was what I would have to do when I came to where larger tributaries entered the river.

I need not have been concerned, however; where a considerable stream entered the Shannon, I only had to detour a few hundred yards 'inland', and return back to the river bank again. The drainage ditch on the 'inland' side of the dyke had water about 1.5m below that of the Shannon, so when a tributary joined the river, the embankment had to follow it upstream to maintain the level.

Opposite the southern tip of Ballymacegan Island I passed a deserted boat club, and saw, rising out of the flat, featureless horizon ahead the silhouette of a tower-house. As I got nearer I identified it by its Jacobean chimneys as

Derryhiveney Castle, which I had visited a few years before. Standing on a raised platform of ground within the remains of an L-shaped bawn, it is one of the last of the tower-house-type dwellings to be built in Ireland, and possibly one of the last truly defensive castles erected in western Europe. The quality and richness of stone-carved decoration, particularly that of the door and window surrounds, was impressive, but I found that the building incorporated two innovations, one an improvement on previous tower-houses, and the other a mysterious disimprovement. There were four great fireplaces in the castle, part of the original construction rather than inserted clumsily afterwards as is the case with most other buildings of the type. The survival of many of the tower-houses in the Irish countryside is due to the comprehensive structural use of stone. Where timber was incorporated, it was rarely built into walls but allowed to stand free in ventilated space, thus inhibiting rot. In Derryhiveney, however, this good practice was reversed: timber was used for lintels rather than stone, and rather than mounting floor beams on stone corbels projecting from the walls, some are built in, a recipe for eventual disaster.

The next island I drew level with was called Long Island, well-named because it took such a long time to pass by it. Snipe were becoming very common along the reed-bed river margin now, giving their pathetic squeal as they were flushed and went jinking on ahead; if there were two together, they invariably escaped in opposite directions, instinctively doubling their chances to survive being shot. After Long Island Portland Island filled the Shannon before the river ran wide and straight towards Portumna, the first visible sign of which was the sun glittering off a great fleet of cabin cruisers moored at the wharf at Portumna Bridge.

About 1km before reaching the bridge I came across another stream entering the river but after only a short diversion a handy footbridge brought me back to the Shannon, and ten minutes later I had reached the public road. The previous bridge at Portumna was designed and built in 1796 by the Bostonian architect Lemuel Cox, who had just completed the first bridging of the Suir at Waterford. While the Waterford bridge lasted until 1912, the Portumna example, constructed in timber in the same manner, was very dilapidated by 1818 when it was repaired by the ubiquitous Scottish engineer, Alexander Nimmo, but it had to be replaced in 1841. The present bridge, constructed of iron, was built in 1910.

One would be forgiven to think that Portumna is 'on' the Shannon, but it is a long 1.5km slog uphill into the town from the river, and I was relieved and a little footsore when I finally reached the main street. Here I made contact with the local hackney man, and had only a few minutes to wait before he turned up in a mini-van to drive me back to Banagher, where I stayed the night.

From Portumna to Gort,
County Galway

The next town of any significance was Gort, close to the borders with County Clare, and to get there I would have to cross the Slieve Aughty Mountains. The total distance to Gort from Portumna by the route I had planned was about 45km, and since there was little availability of overnight accommodation along my route, I divided it into three stages, and made arrangements with the hackney driver in Portumna to be picked up at the end of each day. The Slieve Aughtys, which cover an area of about 140 square miles, stretch about sixteen miles in a north-west to south east direction, and are not so much mountainous as a series of hills, with the highest point reaching 378m. The name Aughty is said to derive from Echtghe, a magician lady of the Tuatha de Danann who married a servant of Fergus Lusca, king of Connaught. The range was well-described by John Stevens who travelled over it with a Jacobite force in 1690, as follows:

At Scarriff begins one of the most desert wild barbarous mountains that I ever beheld, and runs eight miles outright, there being nothing to be seen upon it but rocks

156

and bogs, no corn, meadow, house or living creature, not so much as a bird. Nothing grows but a wild sedge, fern, and heath. In wet winters this way is absolutely impass-able, in dry summers it is a soft way, but at best in many places very boggy, so that at no time cannon or heavy car-riages can pass that way. Meat was as scarce as other necessities, but that we might not be destitute of all, Providence had furnished a small brook which, though foul and ill tasted by reason of rain and bog, afforded us plenty of drink.

In place of dramatic summits and spectacular scenery Slieve Aughty possesses an immense sense of solitude. The range is surrounded by places where evidence of a prehistoric past is plentiful, and it is very possible that the heights them-selves were inhabited in the Neolithic period. The lack of pla-cenames, however, suggests that little has happened here since the peat bogs, that cover the tops, developed other than the planting of the great swathes of conifers which took place early in the second half of the twentieth century.

It was a hazy but warm morning when I walked out of Portumna and into Portumna Forest Park. The centrepiece of the park is Portumna Castle, a great fortified house erected about 1618 by Richard Burke, 4th earl of Clanricard, and his wife, Frances Walsingham, Countess of Essex. She was the widow of Robert Devereaux, notable Elizabethan soldier and courtier who was for five months in 1599 Lord Lieutenant of Ireland, but secret negotiations he had with The O'Neill were discovered by Elizabeth, and he was executed for treason in 1601. The Burkes were originally the de Burgos, who came to Ireland with Prince John on his wild oats-sowing, tear-away tour in 1185. As the Lords Clanrickard, they were

praised in the song 'The West's Awake':

> ... and glory guards Clanrickards grave,
> Sing Ho! They died their land to save
> 'Neath Aughrim's slopes and Shannon's wave.

The castle was a most advanced and radical design for its time, displaying architectural thinking that could easily be regarded as belonging to the eighteenth or nineteenth centuries. A massive linear central core divides the building into two main compartments and carries the chimneys for a large number of fireplaces. The only visible defensive measures in the building are well-placed musket loops with wide fields of fire in the corner turrets.

The Earl of Clanrickard is said to have never passed a night in his castle, however, not an uncommon occurrence in those days, reflecting the enormous wealth of the English landowners and their absentee habits. Subsequent descendants, however, did occupy the place and in spite of a number of sieges it was lived in continuously by the family until it was gutted by an accidental fire in 1828. The later Clanrickards were enormously rich and the annual income from rents of their extensive lands during parts of the nineteenth century was said to be more than the King himself earned. The Marquess of Clanrickard who inherited the Portumna estate in 1874 is still referred to by the people of the area as the meanest man in the world. When he succeeded to the title he left Ireland to live in London, never returning to his estates, which amounted to 52,000 acres with 1,900 tenants, and he neglected his responsibilities as a landowner. When a series of bad seasons struck farming in Ireland and many landlords reduced their rents to allow their tenants to survive, Clanrickard's rents remained the same, causing great hardship and considerable emigration. In 1886 those tenants who had survived refused to pay rents until they were reduced, and a large number were forcibly evicted by a force of 500 constables, with 75 facing imprisonment.

The castle some years ago came into the possession of the state, and Duchas are close to completing major restoration work.

A local man, obviously out for a walk, stopped beside me to gaze across at the castle. He complained about the great expense of restoring the building, while they could be putting the money into the land hereabouts, to help out the descendants of the people that had suffered so much under Clanrickard.

'It'll be marvellous though when it's finished,' he said as he continued his promenade of the estate.

I walked on down the avenue through a miasma of wild garlic perfumes, and came to the Portumna Priory, an extensive ruin of a Cistercian foundation. The Dominicans took over in the fifteenth century and remained intermittently until the early eighteenth century. It was used as the local Protestant church from 1788 to 1832 when the new First Fruits church was built in the town. Its most notable feature is the glassless remains of the east window, a graceful and delicate composition of fine limestone tracery, which dates from about 1470 and bears the name of its sculptor, Johanne.

A couple of hundred yards further on I reached the silver waters of Lough Derg, which broadens the Shannon's waters to almost eight miles in width in places and extends 24miles southwards to Killaloe. Yachtsmen who frequent the lough say it is as vicious as the open sea in a storm, when biting gales blow in from the Atlantic Ocean and are funnelled out over the lough by way of the estuary of the Scarriff River.

Legends tell of a famous harpist-poet called Ahirny, who travelled the royal courts of Ireland, composing songs and poems about the prowess of the warriors and the wisdom of the rulers. Indeed, the sharpness of his wit and the cut of his sarcasm was feared by all as much as his praise was sought. On a visit to the shores of Lough Derg, he took a dislike to Eochy Mac Luchta, king of south Connaught, who had in his youth lost one of his eyes in battle. Mac Luchta did everything in his power to make the poet's visit comfortable, and as Ahirny was leaving, he offered him anything he could wish for as a gift. The cruel Ahirny demanded the king's eye, and true to his word, Mac Luchta plucked it out and handed it over. The king was taken to the shore to wash the blood from his face and empty socket, and the surface of the whole lake became red. When told of this, the king ordained that from then on the lake would be known as Lough Deargerc, or the Lake of the Bloody Eye.

There were about a dozen cruisers moored in the little harbour but no sign of life. The great lake stretched off southwards into the mist, and the east side was no more than a smudge of grey-blue on the horizon. I left the harbour behind and followed a track into the forest park, the air full of early morning birdsong. To my right the floor of the forest was carpeted with a white sea of wild garlic, and beyond the beech and oaks I occasionally caught glimpses of the castle. To the left a wild swampy marsh margined the lake. In minutes the track became a causeway raised a metre over the swamp, which glistened with dark pools in the midst of the foliage.

I came out of the trees into a vast harvested area of coniferous forest, the track I was following stretching across it for a half mile at least, a good example of what not to do when felling in an amenity forest. The only high point walking across this battlefield was the sight of a herd of about fifteen small deer, fallow I think, which, if they had stayed still would have completely escaped my notice but once one turned and bounded away, white target bobbing, they all followed, a beautiful sight to behold.

Eventually I was back in the trees again, and came to the forest park car park. From here I had to find a way to the main road from Portumna to Gort and found a path wending its leafy way through old woodland but generally heading in the right direction. Blackbirds screeched at me from the safety of thick shrubs, and wrens ticked continuously at my invasion on foot of their world.

A wooden footbridge brought me over a dried-up stream and the path wove its way through a series of still ponds and out of the trees to deposit me at the edge of a golf course. The contrast was startling, from the gentle chaos of the woodland to the openness of the rolling man-made hillocks of mani-cured grass. Re-entering the trees again I came across a sea of bluebells, a scene like the illustration on the lid of a chocolate box, a woodland floor painted with the flowers, a blue mist of colour. The visual thrill was equalled by that to my olfac-tory sense and in spite of the early hour, the air was full of heady bluebell perfume. The great old beeches of the wood, not yet in full leaf, were like fossilised dinosaurs, stretching their arms protectively over the flowers of the forest floor.

Soon, far too soon, I emerged onto the public road west of Portumna, and ran the uncomfortable gauntlet of 2km of noisy speeding traffic. I hurried along hugging the ditch, and was relieved to reach my turn-off up a side road towards Gortamunera. I slowed down and enjoyed the winding nar-row road, a sleepy suburb of Portumna, with not a sign of life in any of the houses, in spite of the fact it was nearly mid-morning.

Ascending gently I came to the crossroads at Gortanummera, overlooked by a grand limestone-faced schoolhouse built in 1860, and sensitively extended. Up to the right a tall stone church with an imposing bell tower occupied a site with grand and extensive views to the west and south. Wandering around its grounds I came upon the verger who was actually tending the grass verges.

'It was originally a Protestant church,' he told me in

answer to my query about its history, 'and was taken down stone by stone in the 1930s where it originally stood in Ballygar, brought here and put back together again. Every stone was numbered!'

He unfortunately knew no more about the circumstances but invited me to view the inside, which was 'nicer inside than out'. Indeed it had a beautiful interior, with exposed timber roofbeams and a wonderful stained glass gothic window forming the reredos.

I continued westwards, standing in as frequent traffic passed. The fields around were occupied by healthy-looking cattle, and at one place a herd of young heifers came thundering up to the hedge to view me, each with bright yellow tags in both ears. As I passed a cowshed an open door gave me a view of a milking machine humming away, but, apart from the verger at Gortunumera and people in cars, I had not seen a soul since leaving Portumna. The smell of warm milk straight from the cow, blended with that of liquid cow dung draining out of the cowshed, strangely not an unpleasant combination, brought me back to the past as only smells can do, to a tiny cowshed in County Waterford where as a child I watched Tom Hayes milking his three cows. I would dodge laughing as he in fun would now and then turn an udder at me and squirt a stream of milk.

The air was full of birdsong, a continuous symphony of calls, among which I could only identify the blackbird, wren and robin. Swallows roller-coastered, diving and swooping along in front of me, hoovering up insects. I found myself listening carefully, however, for the sound of a car, and was always ready to jump into the hedge. I was already regretting choosing this particular route. The cars did not slow down when they saw me on the narrow road, rather they kept bearing down on me only to swerve out around me at the last minute. Almost without exception, the drivers waved a greeting.

Twenty minutes from Gortunumera I crossed over the substantial Killcrow River which rises a few kilometres east of the town of Loughrea and flows into Lough Derg. In the hazy conditions of the day the horizon was but four broad fields away. A sign indicated that Kilcorban Priory was a mile to the right. It was one of the rare establishments to escape, at least initially, the suppression of religious houses during the time of Henry VIII, due to its connections with the Dominican Priory at Athenry, which was protected by a special Act of Parliament. It was for many years the burial place of the Earls of Westmeath, and at least one bishop, Thady Keogh, Bishop of Clonfert, who died in 1687, was buried there.

Beside McDonagh's pub in Tooreen I was surprised to find a very good mini-market with a good range of stock including fresh fruit and wines. I bought some fruit, and in answer to my query, she told me Duniry was five miles on.

I passed another few farms from which the hum of milking machines emanated but still there was no sign of a farmer. There were as many derelict houses as there were new ones; I suspect the derelict ones represented the flight from the land, and the new ones were residences of those who worked in the town. In keeping with the derelict dwellings was the large amount of discarded agricultural machinery rusting on the field margins and in the roadside hedges amidst wild strawberries, primroses and white-flowered deadnettle, from old-fashioned mangles and harrows to more modern wheelless JCBs and upturned tractors.

Away over to the left the unmistakable roof-form of a tower-house came into view on the horizon, which I took to be Pallas Castle, a place I had attempted unsuccessfully to get in to see on a previous reconnaissance. I had heard, however, that Duchas had taken it over and were carrying out renovations, so decided I would see if I could persuade those on the site to let me look around. Opposite a fine gate lodge with curved corners and Roman arched windows I turned down a gravelly lane hoping it was the right one, and after ten minutes came out in the open with the castle standing a short distance ahead. I walked down to a Duchas site hut to ask permission to have a look. In spite of signs of very recent occupation, however, there was no one there, so in the absence of any signs prohibiting me from entering, I gave myself permission and went on.

Pallas is yet another of the castles built in this area by the de Burgos. It eventually came into the hands of the Nugents and is a text book example of how the 'gentry's' way of living evolved over the four centuries after 1400. Fully fortified castles were secure until gunpowder and artillery became common but they were damp, dark and cramped, and as soon as the political situation became calmer at the beginning of the seventeenth century and people became more civilised, it became the fashion to build, often attached to the original castle or within the bawn, a new, more spacious and more decorative dwelling, but one which was still defensible against poorly armed rabble and disgruntled peasantry. Later again, if the fortunes improved by the middle of the eighteenth century, yet another, more comfortable and modern house was built nearby, often of palatial proportions. Here at Pallas the original castle still has its bawn complete with wall walks and parapets and there are the remains of the fortified house built in the Jacobite period against one of the bawn walls. The eighteenth-century house, designed by William Leeson for Anthony Nugent, 4th Lord Riverston, and built nearby in about 1798 but demolished some time after 1934, when the Nugents sold the land. As often is the case, this house was survived by its late eighteenth-century gate lodge, the quality of which gives an indication of what the house might have been like. The last dwelling built on the site, an undistinguished Victorian house, stands before the gates and will probably become a museum associated with the castle. There is also a great overgrown walled garden and what must have originally been a large fish pond near the castle, well worth preserving.

It was good to walk these quiet ruins on my own; I could use my imagination without distraction, something I find hard to do in places thronged with tourists. Although like many such ruins Pallas has been somewhat 'sanitised' by the restoration work of Duchas, there is enough of the original left to get a good sense of the place and how it was in days gone by.

Resuming my journey, I turned off the road which led into the village of Tynagh and walked down a very pleasant winding road towards Duniry, bordered on one side by a stone wall which must have surrounded the original Pallas estate. Behind the wall was a long row of chestnut trees decorated with creamy candleabras of flower. It was obviously a little-used road compared to the one I had left, and the hedges were considerably richer in herb and flower species. Hart's tongue ferns and lady ferns were delicately unfurling themselves in the midst of bluebells and violets, and great clumps of stitchwort illuminated the earthen banks. Stitchwort is an unromantic name for such a pretty bright flower, the juices of which were believed to cure stings (*stich* is the German for string) but its Latin name, *stellaria*, is far more expressive and descriptive.

I past a couple of rare traditional cottages, one of which, with a large fairy bush and a grazing donkey, could have been a typical hand-coloured John Hinde postcard. The road came out into the open on Lackbaun Hill, which, although only about 20 or 30m higher than the surrounding country, seemed to tower above it. I was almost beginning to believe that no one lived in east Galway when I met my first person since Tooreen. A middle-aged man came strolling towards me, and we stopped to exchange pleasantries. He told me that Duniry was about 500m on and commented that it was getting warm.

'It was thundery there for a while,' he said. 'Are you hiking?'

I told him I was heading west towards Ballyvaghan, to which he replied, 'So you're going to do that today?' and we laughed together.

He asked where I was from, a standard query in the countryside, and I told him I was from Dublin, but it was great to be out of the city in the perfumed air of the countryside.

'I found it very quiet along the roads here,' I said. 'You are the first person I have met since Portumna, and all the houses seem empty'.

'They're all out working,' he replied. 'That's the way it is, men and women both, working to pay for the houses and feed the family. Everything has changed in recent years. There's very few left in farming. You have to have a big acreage to make it work. I have 70 acres of land, which was great to make a living on in the 1960s and 1970s. Nowadays there's no way you can do it. You have to have at least 200 acres. The houses you passed are all owned by young people who work in Galway, Ballinasloe and Nenagh – Nenagh is only 25 miles away – you see we're very central here.'

He told me the pub in Duniry would not be open yet if I was planning on getting refreshments there but I could go left at Duniry to get to Curragh about two miles away, where there is a pub and golf course.

I left him strolling and a little further on a grey cluster of roofs came into view above the trees ahead signifying the hamlet of Duniry. Two large slated but derelict houses at the crossroads suggested it must have formerly been a place of some importance which had fallen into decay. The late Canon Patrick Egan, historian, past president of the Galway Archaeological and Historical Society, and author of *The Parish of Ballinasloe*, who I had corresponded with regarding the Shannon embankment, was born here in 1911. I could see no signs or vestiges of the castle here which was occupied in the sixteenth century by the 'Mac Egans and ye Brehons'. The MacEgans were the hereditary Brehon Law scholars of Ireland; they ran a law school at Ballymacegan for the education of Brehon lawyers, an education which could take as many as twenty years to complete. In the fourteenth century one of the MacEgans compiled the legal manuscript called the *Leabhar Breac*.

My legs were stiff from the level walking, which I find much more taxing then climbing, and I stopped to enjoy the pleasure of giving them a stretch.

Duniry was nearly 20km from Portumna on the route I had taken, and I had intended to call a hackney from here to take me back, but the pub was still closed and there was no mobile signal, so I decided to walk south west to Curragh and phone from there.

At Carrowcrin I found a pottery shop run by an Englishwoman who had come to Ireland eleven years before.

It was housed in a series of old out-offices beside a tradition-al house set in a wild and colourful informal garden. The pot-tery was wonderful, based on woodland themes, textures and autumn colours. She was a friendly, vivacious woman with red hair and when she saw I was walking she offered me a cup of tea. I asked her if I could have glass of water, and moments later she returned with a pint glass full. I mentioned to her that I had passed a surprising number of houses with swings and slides in the gardens but with no one at home. She told me that she found Ireland a very lonely place; she came from the Manchester area where the villages and towns were full of people on the move at 8am.

'There'd be people in the bread shop buying new bread, people in the paper shop, people on the way to the factories and the mills, there would be a hustle and bustle and a move-ment of people. Here, places like Loughrea are dead, every-one works all week and and at the weekend they don't get up until late in the day.'

I asked her how she had made friends when she came first.

'Oh, I opened a business and got to know a lot of people and I had plenty of people to talk to.'

She talked about her original home in England as a place where people were friendly and would chat to you even if they did not know you.

She felt that Ireland had completely changed since she had come over from England, and people seemed to drink a lot now, and the pubs seemed never to close.

'The women are all at work, and each family has to have two cars. The women don't cook or bake anymore. The older people bake bread, alright. Tourists who come in here ask me where are all the cottages they've seen in the magazines and there's nothing but bungalows.'

'But in defence of those who leave the old house to fall down and build a new one,' I said, 'if your parents lived in an old damp stone cottage, with a bad roof, no insulation ...'

'... And eleven in a bedroom,' she interjected, laughing.

'... And no bathroom, as soon as you could afford it you would leave all that behind and build a spanking new bungalow with heating, insulation and no rats in the thatch.'

I told her that I had only seen one house with vegetables growing in the garden, cabbages, and she said they were probably for the pigs! She had lots of vegetables out the back, and it was obvious she had green fingers as she pointed out the various creepers and shrubs she had planted. She told me her garden was inspired by the woods and she tried to bring the woodland into the conservatory attached to the house; she certainly succeeded. I would have liked to talk more but I reluctantly said goodbye and continued along the road.

Before long I arrived at Curragh West and McCormacks pub and golf course. I found the proprietor touching up the paintwork, and he put his brush away to pour me a pint of shandy. He told me the golf club, which already had 300 members, was having its official opening at the weekend, and the honours were being done by golfer Christy O'Connor Junior and the Kilkenny hurler D.J. Carey, who was also an accomplished golfer. There was still no signal for my mobile phone so I used the public telephone to arrange for a hackney from Portumna to take me back there for the night.

The following morning I started westwards from Duniry again. It was a quiet narrow road, gradually ascending into the hills through land which was getting poorer by the kilometre. Some distance ahead a farmer drove his tractor across the road and stopped to get out. He went into an adjacent field and I wondered what was happening; it seemed extreme to park your vehicle across even a country road. The answer became clear as, out of the nearby field came herd of cows and the farmer, his wife and a child all formed to create a cordon, waving their hands and shouting 'how! how!' to ensure the cattle crossed the road without wavering into another field on the far side.

As soon as the large herd had passed, I continued, getting a smile and a great hallooo! from the farmer. The land on both sides of the road now consisted of poor fields won from boggy, badly-drained uplands, with scatterings of scrub and birch. In the distance I could see higher ground ahead, covered in a blanket of coniferous woods.

Lawlor's Cross, the last outpost of civilisation on this road, was little more than a scattering of buildings with a filling station and a post office. It was already 10.30am and there was no sign of life yet. I continued on, taking an even narrower road which had a 'long acre' up the middle, and which, immediately beyond the cross, began to climb in earnest into the townsland of Kylebrack West. The lush hedges of the land west of Portumna were left behind now, their places taken by Connemara-like dry stone walls and neglected fields filled with great areas of gorse, its yellow blossoms filling the air with heavy coconut scent. The road also was taking on a neglected look with potholes and stretches where the tarmac was almost completely eroded.

A short distance uphill I entered a dense scrubby woodland, a mixture of stunted beech, holly, birch and sitka spruce, and there was no sign that any of the trees, even the spruces, were thriving. The infrequent openings giving a view down to the south revealed a series of low hills also covered with forestry plantations. I plodded on to arrive at a T-junction near an old ruined school house. It was once Aille National School, which a limestone plaque on the gable declared was opened in 1912. I sat a while on a stone and contemplated the place. The Slieve Aughtys are well known for their damp and rain however, and the children might have spent more time on their playtime huddled in the tiny shelter on the wooden bench seat that still survived. Down at the back were the toilets, with cold cement seats perched over a cesspit. I could imagine the misery of it but maybe I was being too soft; the children that survived in this wilderness landscape must have been a hardy bunch, and there is no reason not to believe that the teacher was not a kindly man or woman, who cared for all his or her charges equally.

I gingerly made my way into the building, wary of falling slates, and found that the floorboards had been taken away, and the stove, and the timber sheeting on the ceilings, and it looked as if it would not be long before a storm cleared the rest of the slates off the roof.

I left the old school behind and turned off the public road into the forestry. It was a relief to be away from the road once again, and as if to celebrate with me a cuckoo began to call his summer song nearby. Spruce trees hung out over the track and I had to duck my way through them in places where the wind had pushed them over. It was clear it was not a successful forest, because those trees which had not been blown down were stunted and looked of little commercial use.

The first sign of life I had seen for quite some time, other than the birds which are constant companions, gave me a start. A stoat darted out in front of me, stopped a moment with one forefoot raised to regard me curiously, and then sinuously trotted on across the track and into the undergrowth, his short black-tipped tail in the air. I was delighted with this sighting; the loneliness of these hills was beginning to make itself felt and the stoat was a sign, in spite of the seeming lifelessness of the countryside, that I was anything but alone.

I came out into an open area of harvested forest, where in spite of the poorness of the ground, a new crop of spruce had been planted. For the first time in a while I could again see a few miles to the south, across the other side of the east-west pass which divides the northern range of the Slieve Aughty from the southern. On the far side of the pass stone-walled emerald green fields reached up onto a dull and featureless moorland ridge which reminded me of the Peak District in Derbyshire.

The trees enclosed me yet again as the track wound around north and then west again to deposit me out in the open on a tarmac road, as the cloudy heavy sky was breached by the weak beams of a sun trying to assert itself.

To the north, south and west lay a great extent of moorland wilderness, a sea of heather and scrub grass stretching into the distance to a long, low, sombre horizon of coniferous wood. Beyond, further layers of hazy low hills faded into the distance. I followed the road as it undulated southwards in the company of a line of telegraph poles, some of them leaning as if tired of carrying the single wire strung between them. The silence was almost a solid thing in this desolate place, and it was a relief to hear the familiar call of the cuckoo again, and a joy to have a sighting of the bird, as it came out of the trees behind me, sickle-shaped wings beating hard, mobbed by a couple of sparrows that constantly swooped and dived on it. Eventually the cuckoo landed on the telegraph wire to stand its ground, and the sparrows, weary of their taunting work, flitted away.

The road climbed briefly and then began to descend, passing a grassy track leading off to the right. I had good reason to remember this track well because some years ago, on an early reconnaissance looking for a route across Ireland, I had gone seriously astray, and to this day I am not sure where I actually went that day. I have ever since regarded the Slieve Aughtys with a certain amount of awe and respect.

I was checking out this side of the Slieve Aughty on foot and had run out of water further east. Earlier I had foraged desperately around the nettle-fringed walls of the old school on the offchance there was some kind of tap surviving but all in vain. I had turned off the road to follow this track which the map seemed to suggest would take me through a pass called Francis Gap between Cashlaundrumlahan, at 365m the highest summit of this part of the Slieve Aughty, and another high point to the north at an elevation of 326m.

I was so thirsty I felt like sucking grass. The track took me across a moor of heather dotted with clumps of hazel, and except where hidden by the higher ground of Scalpeen Rock ahead and Cashlaundrumlahan to the south, there were great and long views. Behind me the expanse of Lough Derg was easily identified, shining in the early sunshine, while to the north the flatlands of east Galway stretched far into the distance. Ahead, a sea of conifers covering the uplands stretched from left to right.

Cornflowers and thistles had speckled the trackside with colour, attracting clouds of bright butterflies that fluttered and flittered to and fro. Soon the track had become very boggy, however, and as I reached clumps of trees that were outliers of the dense forestry ahead, it had petered out completely.

I carried on straight across extremely rough and swampy

wooded ground, my pace slowing dramatically the further I went. It was exhausting territory, and I could see myself blundering along, making little or no progress, for the rest of the day. Although I had a compass and knew what direction I should continue heading, there was danger that I could eventually get myself into terrain so difficult that to go forward or back would be exhausting. And there was something about these lonely uplands that was much more threatening than the most rugged mountains I have climbed. I had eventually come to the conclusion that there was no point continuing, and I reluctantly retraced my steps to a branch track, following it for a further ten minutes, hoping it would turn west. It too came to an end. I did the same with another branch going south, with the same result. There was nothing for it but to return to the road and seek another route westwards. When I look at the modern map of the area I had blundered around in, I have to wonder where I did actually get to. According to the map the area is criss-crossed with forestry roads, and there is a good public road a little more than 2km on from where the forestry road ran out. It was as if I was caught up in a spell, and was briefly in a parallel universe, where the wilderness had no tracks or roads.

I did eventually find a way over the hills, and night was falling when I got to the main road between Loughrea and Gort, thoroughly exhausted and dehydrated. I had to thumb a lift the rest of the way. This time I had planned what I hoped would be an easier way to Gort, breaking the journey at Derrybrian North.

I followed the tarmac road down into the valley of the Owenaglanna river, a name which must simply mean 'the river of the glen', where I was pleased to come across a couple of houses surrounded by a few green fields which had been carved out of the bog; I had not seen an inhabited house for 7km. One of them, painted bright orange, clearly had a newcomer in residence, and an orange dog came running out barking at me, but stopped at the gate in a civilised way. I crossed the bridge over the little river, having to duck to avoid flights of swallows which were flying up and down, close to the surface, only interrupting their low-level flights to swoop up over the bridge.

At the top of the next ridge I was opposite Caheranearl, at 344m, one of the highest points of the northern Slieve Aughtys. The road descended again into forestry, and after a short while came out onto the public road at Derrybrian North. From here I was rescued by a friendly hackneyman and delivered to Carton House in Ballynakill, where I was to spend the night.

Ballynakill is an old village strung out along the Portumna to Gort road surrounded by a rich collection of prehistoric sites including a stone circle, a barrow, a *fulacht fiadh* (prehistoric cooking place), megalithic tombs, standing stones and crannógs, all evidence that for at least 4,000 years man has found that this little corner of south Galway a pleasant place in which to live. Unfortunately, at least six important monuments have disappeared during land reclamation in the last century. Marble Hill House, the 'big house' of the area, was built around 1800 by the Burkes, (the de Burgos again) but suffered destruction by burning during the War of Independence. Ann Garnsworthy takes in guests at Cartron House, said to be one of the oldest houses in the area, and it is also a centre for horse-drawn caravan holidays. From the fulsome praise to be found in the visitor's comments book, tourists from all over the world have found Cartron and Ballynakill a particularly peaceful place to spend time.

Among those staying when I was there was a young honeymoon couple from England, who, taking pity on me eating on my own, insisted I join them at their table for dinner. They were Londoners, and were enjoying a few days on a cruiser on the Shannon, and some time wandering from Cartron House in a horse-drawn caravan. They were interested in going to the pub after dinner, and I almost succumbed. Although I had not covered a great amount of ground that day, I was really tired, and concerned to keep whatever energy I had remaining for the last three stages to Ballyvaghan, so I slipped away to bed at 9.30.

Twelve hours later Ann Garnsworthy dropped me back in Derrybrian North, and I set off into the forest. It was drizzling rain from a low cloud ceiling but I had had a great night's sleep and was feeling full of energy and ready for anything. I had 22km ahead of me which would take me over the last hills of the Slieve Aughty and down nearly 300m to the low-lying town of Gort.

Within minutes of hearing Ann's car receding into the distance the silence and the deep sense of solitude I had experienced the previous day descended on me again as I followed the forestry road gently uphill. The morning birdsong of the previous couple of days was absent, perhaps because of the later hour or the wet weather. As I got deep into the plantation, however, a familiar call rang through the trees. A relay of cuckoos had seemed to follow me the previous day and now the next in line started his song, as if to remind me that I must be mad to walk through this bleak place.

The Derry part of the placename Derrybrian, as in County Offaly, means that there was once oakwoods here. Indeed, I am told there is plenty of evidence in the area, in the form of old iron workings and tanneries, to suggest that all

of these oakwoods had been used up by these industries by Tudor times. The quick-growing conifers that now clothe the place in a thick, impenetrable jungle, interspersed with areas of wet bogland are a poor replacement for the one-time mighty oak forest, but indicate one of the reasons why the native Irish found it possible to resist cultural domination for centuries when they took to the hills. To try to bring a medieval army through such landscape in search of rebel clans was an extraordinarily difficult task, as many foreigners found. I know by experience that even today there is no way over the Slieve Aughtys other than to follow the forestry roads; I hoped my map was correct this time and that the line I had chosen would take me all the way.

The drizzle died out and it became quite warm, so taking off my waterproofs and tucking them into my rucksack, I strode out again, feeling fresh and comfortable. In spite of the thick wall of trees on both sides, it was a pleasant, if a little monotonous, winding road with few long straights. The monotony gave the occasional open glades great importance, like one where a stream was bridged, and I found myself pausing to enjoy the visual relief, standing a while gazing into the peaty waters.

One little incident took on the importance of a major event. A hare came out of the trees some 12m ahead and trotted towards me. I stopped dead and stood still. He continued to approach, his long rear legs seeming quite awkward at slow speed. About 8m away he paused as if sensing something was wrong. His ears twitched and his nose quivered. His big glistening doe-like eyes were looking straight at me, and although I knew hares have bad eyesight, I could not believe he could not see me, dressed as I was in clothes of a colour that contrasted significantly with my surroundings. Yet he trotted on again towards me again, slower this time, to stop within 6m. His ears were like antennae, and his nose sniffed the air furiously, while he turned his head to look at me first with one eye, and then with the other. Finally, he seemed to decide that all was not well, and he turned round, trotting slowly back the way he had come. Then, as if he suddenly realised what he had seen, he gave a frenzied leap ahead, and ran like only hares can do, at terrific speed, back up the track and out of sight.

The cutting for the forestry road showed the depth of the

peat to be around half a metre, but as I passed near the high-est point of the hill there were places where the bedrock of the Slieve Aughtys burst through the earth and peat. In one place some primordial convulsion of the earth heaved one section of the bedrock up above the surrounding ground, revealing a cross section showing a thin shaley layer overly-ing the earlier rock, pink old red sandstone. This outlier of the sandstones was laid down more than 300 million years ago and dominates the geology of the south and southwest of Ireland, making up the Macgillicuddy Reeks, the Galtees, the Knockmealdowns and the Comeragh mountains.

As the track began to descend, the surface deteriorated to a moss-covered quagmire with a line of rushes down the mid-dle, and I began to wonder would the track, contrary to what the map suggested, run out and leave me again faced with an impenetrable wall of trees. A little farther on, however, the track improved again, although churned up by forestry machinery, and I came across a vast area of harvested forest. Here the track was lined with a huge 'clamp' of cut logs, the size of a 40m-long terrace of houses, a vast timberland sculp-ture.

Beyond this the track was newly surfaced and it swung south, reaching the perimeter of the plantation near Keelderry, or Oakwood, and I found myself on a tarmac bog road crossing open moorland stretching as far as the eye could see. I had promised myself a refreshment stop after two hours of walking, and as I came to a stone-walled bridge over a little stream, I unslung my rucksack and sat down. It was glorious to take off my boots and rest my feet in the damp grass, reminding myself of a similar sojourn on the top of Rathmore in County Kildare nearly 130 miles back.

After such a time enclosed by forest, I found the views,

although hazy, a great delight. Back in the direction from which I had come I could see, above a dull green layer of trees, the highest point of these hills, Cashlaundrumlahan but the best view was to the south. Out of the mist in that direction, about 9km away across the border in County Clare, Lough Graney shone like dull silver, a single large island in its centre. Further west was another body of water which I guessed was Lough Cutra. I sat gazing into the distance, serenaded by skylarks and meadow pippits, and then put my boots back on before setting off again.

Soon the road began to descend, and I gazed towards the horizon hoping to see the town of Gort, but in vain. As the descent became steep and winding, a tractor came uphill and passed me, the driver returning my wave though looking surprised to see someone walking down from the bog. The road was now bounded by informal hedgerows of birch, holly, elder and gorse, and I soon after came across the first dwelling of the day, a neat tin-roofed, whitewashed cottage, gable to the road. By the cleanliness of the yard and the navy blue-painted woodwork, I took it to be a foreigner's retreat, and a few metres further on, in the haggard of the cottage, I found the proof of this. Over a low wall was an enclosure occupied by two fat ewes and three healthy-looking lambs. One of the ewes had a bell around her neck, which clonked like a Tyrolean cow-bell as she came towards me, followed by the other ewe and the lambs. The lambs put their noses up to me to be rubbed, baa-ing all the time, and posed politely for a photograph. I did not think these could have been the animals of an Irish farmer.

On downhill I went into the townsland of Hollymount, where I stopped to sit on a a felled tree at the roadside and have a light lunch. The weather forecast had said it would 'brighten up later' and indeed it did. The sun came out as I ate a delicious repast of dried apricots, wholemeal biscuits and chocolate, washed down with coffee. I was almost halfway to Gort now, and as I knew I would be on tarmac for the rest of the day, I exchanged my boots for a pair of runners and set off again.

Below Hollymount the road followed a small verdant river valley scattered with well-kept cottages. High hedgerows of holly and hawthorn sheltered a glorious variety of herbs and wildflowers, including fraughans, hartstongue ferns, wild strawberries, mosses, wood sorrel and violets, and as I progressed, bluebells, primroses and early purple orchids. After the paucity of species in the coniferous forest above, this road was a treasurehouse. One farm had an entire trained hedge of snowberry shrub, a few hundred metres long, something I have not seen before.

I passed reed-fringed Lough Avalla, with its glass-calm waters, before reaching a cross roads to the left of which my map told me was a cillín, or infant's graveyard. In such places infants who died without baptism or stillborn babies were interred in time gone by, though in more primitive parts of the country the practise only died out 50 years ago. I went in search of the place and met a young woman on the road with a child by the hand, watching her farmer husband manhandling straw bales in the nearby field. When I asked about the cillín, she said she thought it was further on, 'in the land'. She called her husband over and I asked if there was much to see of it.

'No, no,' he said, 'there's only a few stones stickin' out of the ground.'

'Was there a wall around it?' I asked.

'Ah, there was, but its all gone now.'

It seemed clear he had little interest in either the cillín, the stones of the wall of which he had probably used himself, or of me coming onto his land to look at it, so I thanked them and continued on my way.

After a long straight stretch of road I passed the first of a succession of suburban type houses, a sign I was approaching the town of Gort. Almost invisible at the roadside under vigorous early summer growth, I noticed a covered well with a wrought iron gate. As my water bottle was almost empty I decided to fill it, and using my stick as a machete to beat down the grass and ivy, I descended a couple of steps and wrenched the gate open to reveal a dark pool of water. Waterboatmen scurried away, and there was a scattering of duckweed on the surface reminding me of the well near my cottage in Waterford, but the water was crystal clear, and tasted beautiful.

Farther on I searched for a holy well that was marked on my map, and just before giving up, I found an overgrown stile over the stone roadside wall. It led me through an arboreal tunnel under an overgrown copse of scrub to a rough circle of stones in the middle of which was a spring. There were no offerings or coins to suggest that this well had been frequented in recent years, and it looked like it would disappear altogether before long. I found it disappointing to think that the prosperity which is sweeping the country is also in danger of sweeping away important local sites such as the cillín, the utility well and the holy well, all important reminders of Ireland in another age.

A girl I met told me, in answer to my query about the holy well, that she thought it was called Tobar MacDuagh, named for the saint who founded the monastic centre at Kilmacduagh, a few miles south of Gort.

I ran the gauntlet of a short stretch of main road before getting onto what appeared to be a very old boreen at Kinicha, bounded by dry stone walls running parallel to the river Annagh into Gort. On the horizon ahead I got my first glimpse of the hills of the Burren, which but for the haze I should have been able to see much earlier from the slopes of the Slieve Aughty. It was a thrill to see those grey-blue cloud-like hills under which I would end my odyssey. My glimpse of the promised land increased my haste and with renewed energy, I quickened my pace. In the near distance the first buildings of Gort appeared, a church spire rising above a series of grey slated roofs.

The boreen crossed a railway line and then dropped down close to the river, a pleasant stretch with views across to the far bank where cattle and horses grazed the water-meadows like a scene out of Constable's England. The beauty of this was suddenly and dreadfully contrasted as the boreen led into what seemed to be a chaotic tip-head, opposite some industrial buildings surrounded by waste materials and a wire fence festooned with wind-blown plastic. It is a shame, in this age of supposed enlightenment, that such a fine approach to the town of Gort has been allowed to come to this. A large sign stated

No Dumping
£1,500 Fine
or 1,904.61 Euro
By Order

The lane led me past the old station onto the main street of Gort, which reminded me of the description of Gort written in 1814 by the aptly-named John Trotter, a pedestrian traveller:

> We reached the town of Gort to breakfast. It is approached by a fine avenue of trees – always to us a welcome sight. It is a neat modern town, containing nothing remarkable. As we were anxious to make a long walk this day, we hurried on, disappointing the curious gaze of several in this country-town, who, as is too customary in Ireland, having little business to occupy them, are devoured with curiosity to know that of others. Pedestrians of a genteel appearance very much puzzle these characters; and as there are no servants to question, – no equipages to examine – and no postilions to listen to, these persons are left in suspense.'

I made my way to the Lady Gregory Hotel where I was booked in for the night. As I entered the gateway of the hotel rain began to fall, and by the time I walked through the door a torrential downpour was in progress, and shattering peals of thunder split the air. There was a power cut in the hotel, and the receptionist apologised that unless the electricity came back cold food only would be available that evening. I climbed the two storeys to my room, where I found a spacious queen-size bed. The sense of luxury when, after a shower, I stretched out on the vast bed, is indescribable.

From Gort to Galway Bay at Ballyvaghan, County Clare

I rose early and, opening the curtains of my room, was greeted by a clear day, with the sun well up over the Slieve Aughtys, which were visible from my second-floor room as a hazy smudge along the eastern horizon. I was the first down for breakfast in the vast dining room of the Lady Gregory, but it was not long after I had tucked into my 'full Irish' that the room filled with two coach loads of elderly German tourists. Up to a couple of years ago the only hotel in Gort was Glynns, an old-world, dark place with deep red carpets long past their best, exuding a not unpleasant miasma of drink and cigarettes. Probably originally a town house, it was not very commodious, and there were few rooms en suite. The lunches they served in the bar, great steaming plates of Galway lamb, carrots, cabbage and mountains of mashed potatoes, were prodigious. The bar itself was tiny, probably once a reception room of the house, and had walls decorated with a mixture of old prints and fine modern photographs of the Burren. Clearly Glynns was not in a position to attract the coach loads of tourists a real hotel needs to survive today, and it sadly went out of business around the time the Lady Gregory opened.

The Lady Gregory is but one of a large number of similar hotels that have sprung up since the late 1990s when Ireland began to become a rich country worth investing in. The decor of their day-rooms is similar; contemporary baronial might be a description with lots of natural wood, painted panel ceilings, timber floors, stained-glass swing doors, and double height spaces, with familiar prints of internationally-known Irish writers. The bedrooms are spacious and comfortable, and in the bathrooms the one feature which I really appreciate, the power shower.

My plan for the day was to reach the Burren and climb a couple of the eastern hills to a rendezvous point where I had arranged to be picked up by an old friend, Dick Cronin.

I set out through the town, and paused on the bridge over the Annagh river to reflect on hoardings advertising extensive apartment schemes for Gort, which has a population of about 1,200. On the north of the main street was a tattered poster showing an aerial view of an ambitious riverside scheme which must have come to grief; the site beyond was an overgrown wasteland. On the south side of the street was a new colourful poster advertising another scheme, which seemed to be well under way. I wondered what had gone wrong with the earlier scheme; was it too early, perhaps, before the confidence brought by the Celtic Tiger had percolated to south Galway? From the bridge there is a fine view of the extensive buildings and gardens of the Convent of Mercy, the core of which was once Lord Gort's residence in the town. I could not help wondering how long it would be before this site too would come under the auctioneer's hammer.

Farther on was the closed Glynn's Hotel, where virginia

creeper had all but shrouded the cut-limestone façade, windows and all. An old brass frame beside the door advertised Molly Glynn's Bar with a 1930s-style graphic of a stylised glass of wine, a plate, fork and napkin, and the door bore a notice of a planning application for retention of the façade, but demolition of the rear of the hotel and the construction of a new bedroom block. Glynn's, it seems, will live on. I walked through the square past the Arches Bar, where I took part in a Fleadh Ceoil some years ago.

Just outside the town I passed through a suburbia of large modern houses in manicured gardens, fronted by dark limestone walls, which, are insisted upon by the Planning Department. I can understand they want to encourage more use of local materials, but more flexibility and creativity is needed in the boundary requirements of the planning department, including allowing or even conditioning the retention of existing hedgerows, giving a natural, informal rural variety to the roadsides.

Before long I left the suburbs of Gort behind, passing a series of metal box-type factory buildings and noting that even here in this south Galway farmer's town there was modern industry. Reaching the brow of a low hill I saw the hills of the Burren come into sight ahead. I had seen them vaguely the day before entering Gort but now they stretched from north to south, long, low-lying layers of cloud-dappled grey. I turned onto a road which I am told is still called 'The New Line', in spite of the 500 years that have elapsed since it was built by colonising Anglo-Normans. The road headed straight for nearly 2km towards the Burren hills, through an Anglo-Norman townsland called Newtown.

In a field to the left I passed an island of dense thorn and hazel which, my map suggested, hid vestiges of the old

Killura graveyard, which is said to have a number of old gravestones bearing the name of the local clan chieftains, the O'Shaughnessys. Averil Swinfen, in her excellent book on the Burren churches, *Forgotten Stones*, relates that an elderly resident of Gort reported some years ago that he had found two grave stones there dated 1575, covering the remains of the 'Queen's O'Shaughnessys', two members of the clan who supported Elizabeth I and were not allowed to be buried in the family tomb at Kilmacduagh.

Tom Hannon, a local historian, told me that 'The New Line' road had been built by the Normans in summertime, much to the amusement of the locals, because it crosses a turlough which floods in winter, making the road impassable. The water level in the turlough was quite low as I paused at a bridge over a stream to look out over what remained of Newtown Lough or Lough Nacarriga, its old name, which means simply the lake of the rocks. The stream meandered alongside a stone wall through a field of bright new grass to the exquisitely still waters of the turlough, which is a Gaelic word that has become part of the English language. The landscape I was now entering contains more turloughs that any place in Ireland; Rahasane turlough a few miles to the northeast is the largest in Ireland, a flat prairie of 275 hectares of grassland that in wintertime becomes a great lake which attracts over 40,000 wildfowl. One or more swallow holes fill and drain turloughs, and they can fill up very fast; frequently autumn campers who have selected what they thought was a dry grassy field to camp in have woken to find themselves, and all their gear, afloat.

A little farther on I came to a gateway leading to Newtown Castle, which I was told was worth a visit. I walked down a causeway-like road to the ivy-covered structure said to have been built by Irehemias Follane in the middle of the sixteenth century. It is an unusual circular castle; although circular tower-houses are not uncommon, this had a pronounced batter or inward slope to its walls, and because the top was missing, with its 12m height, it resembled more a Martello tower. Like a cap at a jaunty angle, ivy topped the ruin and hung down its walls to the top of the deep gothic-arched doorway. The cut stone of the doorway, facing as it was towards the north and protected against the worst the sun, rain and wind could do, was as fresh as the day the mason had worked it 500 years before, but a gateway of timber pallets prevented me from entering to explore further.

Back on the road again I headed for the hamlet of Roo, a place which has disappeared completely from recent maps. A number of years ago, when carrying out the initial planning of the cross-Ireland route, I exchanged correspondence with a local historian, Tom Hannon, regarding the paths and roads in the area. I later had the pleasure of meeting Tom, and we had lunch together in Glynn's Hotel, during which he regaled me with the history of the Gort area. What made Tom's interpretation of history special was the importance he gave the ordinary things and ordinary families, as well as the great, and he told it as though it happened only yesterday, which in a way it did. People like Tom make history live and topical. He showed me the old roads in the area and all the places of interest, with constant reference to the people and the families who lived there in times gone by. It was a richly informative experience and I could have easily spent a week wandering with him around the dramatic Punch Bowl, Lough Cutra and Lough Graney, the streets of Gort and all the side roads about. Soon after this Tom and his wife went to the US to visit their daughter, and while they were away subterranean water levels in the low-lying basin west of Gort flooded an extensive area of land, including many houses. Their house was one of those inundated, and such was the damage and the potential for it to happen again, that they were forced, like many others, to move to higher ground and build a new house.

Passing by Tirneevin church I turned down a narrow boreen and after a few minutes came to their beautiful old cottage. On our last visit Tom and his wife had given Teresa and I a feverfew plant, and it still grows in our garden in Dublin. The cottage garden it came from, however, was sadly overgrown now, enveloping what remained of their old cottage. I continued on and after a few minutes came to their new house, a fine bungalow overlooking another turlough, and with a view to the south of the leaning round tower of nearby Kilmacduagh. I had not told them I was coming, and they did not expect me, but nevertheless I was welcomed and in spite of my protestations, a tasty repast was set before me. A most enjoyable hour was spent with Tom and his wife before returning to the road and my journey.

After a bright start the sky had clouded over, and it had taken on a leaden look as I left the townsland of Roo and turned again towards the hills of the Burren, the greys of the limestone pavements ahead on the horizon merging with those of the low clouds. A long, straight road of at least 2km in length led me away from trees and hedgerows quite abruptly into a landscape of dry stone walls dividing fields of bare limestone flags interspersed with patches of herbs and grass. The contrast with the lush fields I had left a short distance behind could not be more dramatic; as far as I could see, to the foot of the hills ahead, stretched a wilderness, a desert of rock, a stark place, beautiful in its harshness. No

wonder Cromwell's general Ireton is said to have commented about this part of Clare that there was not enough water to drown a man, not a tree from which to hang a man, and not enough earth to bury a man. Across the flatness a few stunted, leaning *sceachs*, and in the far distance the tall shape of Dungory Castle, were the only vertical elements in the landscape. John Trotter described, having left Gort, his arrival at this place in 1814 as follows:

> Thus we left our friends at Gort, and passing through some well-wooded places of Mr Gregory and Mr O'Hara, reached a long dreary expanse, which I called 'the plains of desolation' Large fields, if fields they could be called, covered with continuous ledges of rock, spread around us on every side, and before us the solitary ruined castle of Drimisne stood in the midst of this extraordi-

nary and miserable scene. You will not marvel much my dear L., if all we had read and heard of the Irish being driven, by Cromwell's commissioners, and other less barbarous English governors, to this province, rushed into the mind.

Twenty years before Trotter passed the French pedestrian adventurer De Latocnaye said of the Burren:

It would seem that this country has been swept by the ocean in some great convulsion of the globe, and that the covering of earth has in this way been removed. Here are to be seen plains of seven or eight miles long without the least vestige of soil, and without verdure other than that of a few hazel-nut bushes which grow in odd corners among the stones.

Clouds were piling up darkly over the Burren hills, which had turned almost as black as the sky over them. It was clear that if it did rain there would be no shelter for me other than that of the hazel scrub under the first of those hills I would have to cross, a nameless 205m-high, layered dome of almost bare limestone a couple of kilometres ahead. A chill breeze sprung up, an advance guard of the expected rain, creating a hissing sound through the stone walls, and as it did, a lance of sunlight broke through the cloud and reflected off the pavement ahead, creating a surreal scene. I paused to put on my rain jacket and continued.

I hurried along, head down, noting that the violets along the roadside seemed bigger and more violet than those I had seen farther back in the foothills of the Slieve Aughty. Looking over the stone wall as I went I paid more attention to the herbage in the patches of grass between the limestone pavements, and was rewarded with the delightful sight of electric blue spring gentians, a signal that I finally had arrived in the Burren. Ragged pyramids of early purple orchids stood amid golden clumps of bird's foot trefoil, and something I did not expect, a few thick stands of red valerian along the road-side, that lime-loving pink 'weed' that colonises old stone walls and is said to have been brought to Ireland by the Normans.

I looked up from my botanical searches to find that the dark clouds I had thought were heading straight for me had been successfully warded off by my rain jacket, and were dumping curtains of water a few miles away to the south. A lark began to sing melodious praises of my wizardry high above my head. I was surprised to find that I had been fol-lowing the road across the pavements for half an hour, and it seemed more like ten minutes. No matter how often I visit the Burren or read about the place, it is always new and special. Almost as suddenly as the bare pavements had appeared a couple of kilometres to the east, they disappeared from sight again as I progressed under green, luxuriant fields and scrub woodland of holly, birch and mountain ash. The road entered a hazelwood, interrupted only by a clearing in which stood a burnt-out caravan and a wrecked car surrounded by rubbish, a particularly obscene sight in the midst of all the beauty.

Farther on I passed a house in the trees with, at the entrance gate, a carved standing stone decorated with a bud-dha, and a declaration *Lig do scith*. For a moment I thought this was an invitation to come in and take your ease, but realised that it was probably just the name of the house, so I restrained myself and continued on.

My first Burren hill, made up of four distinct layers, with

a rough stone wall climbing to its summit, was looming ahead now. It would have looked daunting but I had walked the Burren many times and found these hills easily climbed. I had planned to follow the wall up the hillside but first had to look for a gap in the thick cordon of scrub hazel bordering the road that would deliver me out on the open pavements. A sign at an easy place said 'No Trespassing', so I was going down the road seeking another suitable place when a young man dressed like the gypsies of old came along on a bike.

'D'ye want to get up the hill?' he called.

'I do,' I said, 'but there's a "no trespass" sign down there'.

'Ah, bollox to that,' he called, 'that's all bollox. Go on in there, just ahead of you, there's a good place,' and he stopped and pointed to a spot which had clearly been often used.

'Nobody will bother you,' he said as he mounted the bike again, and I called 'Thanks' after him as he sped away.

I was nor sure whether it was 'bollox' because the sign meant nothing, or that in a free country one should ignore such signs, but with the man's encouragement I took my chances anyway. Over the wall I went, gingerly, because Burren drystone walls are difficult to climb without bringing them down around and on you, and started up the pavements, feeling great to be off the road once again.

The drystone wall that climbed to the summit looked from the map to be the county boundary between Galway and Clare, and keeping to its north I delayed my entry into Clare as long as possible.

Walking the pavements of the Burren is a very different experience to walking ordinary hills. Burren hills are made up of a series of almost flat shelves, a kind of giant's staircase with the risers of shattered limestone and scree that are steep but easy to scramble up. From below and from a distance it looks as if the hills are composed entirely of bare rock but in fact large areas of the flat parts are well carpeted with grass, as well as being jewelled with herbs and wildflowers. Where the limestone is bare it is crossed by grikes or deep cracks from which emerge a rich variety of Lusitanian and alpine plants and miniature, stunted hazel and thorn bushes. You need to concentrate and keep your eye on your footing to ensure you do not step into a grike and as many of the scattered slabs of limestone are loose and unstable, they sometimes rock alarmingly with a ringing 'clonk' sound as you put weight on them. The English fell-walker Alfred Wainright's maxim for safety on the hills, 'watch where you're going, and stop if you want to look at the view', is very appropriate on the Burren hills. An added advantage of keeping your eyes on the ground is the things you will see, such as delicate corals in the limestones, the sometimes intriguing shapes the water has sculpted the stone into, as well as the violets, the primroses and all the other glorious, colourful herbs.

As I reached the second last shelf from the top, a broad, flat grey-flagged terrace with dark grikes snaking away sinuously southwards like rivers in a fossilised landscape, I paused and sat down to take in the view behind me, the plain since leaving Roo. In the far hazy distance were the uplands of the Slieve Aughty merging greyly with the landscape around Gort, and then a sea of grey pavements stretched towards me, only to give way to green fields and hazel scrub just below the hill I had climbed. About a mile away in the midst of the scrub a cluster of white caravans suggested an encampment of New Agers, probably where the young man who directed me at the base of the hill came from. To the south between the southern Slieve Aughtys and the south eastern Burren,the plain was interspersed with silver-surfaced turloughs. The landscape seemed to be divided equally between barren rock and well-cultivated grassland, much of it in vast fields.

I waited for the sun to emerge to take a good photograph, hunched down in a light drizzle, serenaded by larksong as I nibbled a snack of apricots and wholemeal biscuits. I had time to spare, because I was not due at my pick-up point on Slieve Carran until six o'clock, and it was now only four. After twenty minutes I was out of biscuits and beginning to feel cold, yet although the misty rain had stopped there was no sign of the sun breaking through, so I abandoned the photograph, gathered my belongings and continued towards the top. Ten minutes later I reached the flat plateau-like top of the hill and setting out across the thick grass surface I crossed into County Clare. The grass hid treacherous grikes and had to be negotiated with care, but slowly the landscape west of the hill revealed itself. Straight ahead were the severe grey cliffs of the eastern face of Slieve Carran, at the southern end of which I had arranged to be picked up. Looking to the north west just past the portal of Slieve Oughtmama I was pleased to get my first glimpse of the sea since leaving the Dublin Mountains behind; famous Galway Bay stretched a mottled slate grey and deep blue surface over to the low coastline of County Galway.

After a short crossing of the plateau the ground dropped away abruptly to reveal the thickly wooded valley between the two hills. I knew a road ran up this valley but there was no sign of it, and for a moment I had to check my map again to see if I had gone astray somehow. My map said I was in the right place, and on closer observation I could see a line of telegraph poles rising above the hazel wood below, and

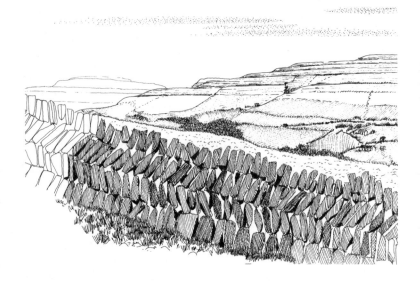

assumed that the road was simply hidden from view.

The descent of the hill with care took longer than the ascent but before long I could see the road. Before reaching it I veered north to see if I could find a holy well that was marked on the map. It did not take long; inside a low-walled triangular enclosure I found a rough structure of lichened slabs, overhung by a great old thorn tree, covering a dry pit.

I reached the road and turned uphill and south through a thick wood of hazel scrub. The hazel leaves were not yet fully out, and for a couple of weeks longer the floor of boulders richly covered with feathery mosses and decorated with bluebells and primroses would benefit from the dappled light of the sun. The scrub wood was interrupted halfway up the hill by an extensive farm with fields of luxuriant grass which had no doubt been wrested from the wilderness. The fields were speckled with pale yellow cowslips, proof not only that fertilisers were not in use here, but of the natural goodness and warmth of the limestone bedrock, which I was told by a Clare farmer can sometimes be only inches below the surface. He also told me that the connoisseur of home-made butter can tell, from the taste of the herbs in the butter, what part of the Burren the cattle which produced the milk had grazed.

I arrived at the little National Park car park where I was to be picked up by Dick a half-hour early, so I crossed the wall and lay down in the wildflower-scented grass with my rucksack as a pillow. A cuckoo was calling somewhere nearby, and I lay, comfortable and warm, watching the dark clouds as they continued to pass slowly overhead, sometimes opening to reveal a little blue, sometimes turning leaden. I must have dropped off, for I awoke with a start when a large raindrop slapped me on the nose. The rain had finally come, and I pulled up my hood and got into the shelter of the road-side wall, for a minute or two before Dick arrived to my rescue in his Landrover.

We went to Monks pub in Ballyvaghan where we had a couple of pints and a meal. It may sound a little peculiar that I was staying the night in the place that I was going to walk to the following day, but I like Ballyvaghan, and I was making the rules! We called into a hotel on the way back to our Bed and Breakfast, and got briefly but enjoyably involved with a crowd gathering for a wedding the following day, before we headed for bed.

The following morning I awoke to find to my delight that the cloudy conditions of the previous day had been banished by a clear blue sky and sunshine that promised a great day for my last stage. County Clare is one of my favourite counties, and the Burren my favourite part of Clare.

I am impressed by the make of the Clare people, truly and uncompromisingly Irish, wearing the culture thoroughly and

easily, particularly the music and dance, but able to assimi-
late other cultures without harming their own, rather enrich-
ing it. Even the young can attend a céili one night, dancing all
the traditional sets with energy and skill, and go to the disco
the following night, enjoying it just as much.

Dick and I met up at 9am with Mary and Jenny, two
members of a Sligo walking club who had driven south to
join us on the traverse of the Burren, the last stage of my
coast-to-coast odyssey. Before long I was heading across the
pavements again, this time with the luxury of company.

The goal for the day was the end of my journey through
the seasons across Ireland, the Atlantic Ocean at
Ballyvaghan. On a previous reconnaissance I had used too
much road to get there, so this time I was going to concentrate on getting as far as I could cross-country, although
because I wanted to visit the monastic site at Oughtmama, I
would still have to include 4km of tarmac. My idea was to go
northwards over Slieve Carran, cross the saddle between it
and Turlough Hill, go west over Turlough and then north
again down to Oughtmama. We would be into farmland
then, so I intended following the public road to access an old
pass between Ailwee and Moneen Mountain which would
take us over and down to Ballyvaghan. The high density in
the landscape of surviving monuments from every epoch of
Ireland's history is something that is unique about Clare in
general and the Burren in particular, and the route I had chosen was no exception I expected it to unfold a feast of historic
riches, as well as geological and botanical delights.

Before climbing onto the plateau, we followed a barely
discernible stone-paved track, parts of it cut from the limestone bedrock, to find St Colman's church, the ruins of a
sixth-century oratory tucked into the hazelwood under Slieve

Carran's tall eastern cliffs. A pair of ravens circled as we made our way into the dense little wood where, on a platform, surrounded by thickly moss-laden trees, stood the sun-dappled remains of an early Christian church. It is a beautiful and peaceful place floored with a tumble of moss-covered rocks, between which a stream draining the heights of Slieve Carran above cascades down. Nearby is a holy well constructed in a circle of stone. All that survives of the church is a solitary cyclopean stone-built gable, its straightness and the alignment of its stones as good as the day it was erected, which makes one wonder what befell the rest. One great stone in the gable turned out on examination to be only 70mm thick, a slab rather than a structural stone the same thickness as the wall. We wondered if it was a panel with saints' relics behind it, and obviously so had a previous visitor, who had created a hole rummaging in the rubble behind it. Much of the wall rests upon it, so if it is moved or further disturbed the whole gable might collapse.

St Colman Mac Duagh is said to have spent seven years here looking out over the Burren, sheltered from the west winds and facing the rising sun, his only companion an acolyte to serve mass for him. No trace of the hermitage he founded here, which would have been built from timber, remains today, of course, but there are vestiges of stone dwellings among the trees that must have housed later monks. The site is still visited frequently, and on St Colman's feast day, 3 February, mass is celebrated on a great slab of rock near the church. The paved trackway we had followed to the church ruin is ancient, and most likely a lot older than the church. The name the road, Bothar na Miasa, or the road of the dishes, has been handed down for nearly fifteen centuries, and relates to a legend about St Colman.

In between fasting it appears that Colman was partial to a good feed, and often dined with the local king, Guaire. At the end of Lent one year he asked his servant if he had prepared anything special for their Easter feast, and was told that the usual nuts, bread and beer were on the menu. The saint meditated on how hard their life was, and how they deserved better, and asked the Almighty to intervene. Five miles away, at the Dun on the site which Dunguaire Castle now occupies, King Guaire was at that moment preparing to begin his Easter feast when the dishes laden with food on the table before him rose up in the air and disappeared out the window. In amazement the king and his retinue gave chase, and followed the flying dishes along the road all the way to Colman's hermitage, where they saw the food come into land before the saint and his servant. Since then the road has been known as Bothar na Miasa.

Reluctant to leave, we spent a while pottering about this beautiful place, the quietness only broken by the cronking of ravens cruising the Cinn Faill cliffs above, and the occasional wren's indignant tirade in the hazel scrub.

We returned a little way along Bothar na Miasa and then left it to climb the southern terraces of Slieve Carran. Spring Gentians, giving off a brilliant blue glow in the sunlight, decorated the grassy herbariums between the pavements, and there were also scatters of white mountain avens and yellow bird's foot trefoil; later in the summer there would be pendulous harebells as well. I found I was not alone in my love of flowers, as Jenny, and Mary in particular joined my ooh-ing and aah-ing about each new clump we encountered. It was a little strange, and very welcome, to have companions to share and discuss sights with, and my pace, after the push of the previous stretches, slowed greatly as I began to relax into my

last day. We stopped again before reaching the top for a breather and an early snack, and spent a considerable time admiring the layered Burren hills all round, the cloud shadows caressing their rounded forms, seeking out and shaping their summits and declivities.

Taking our time like this we took a full two hours reaching the plateau of Carran, a great meadow of long grass with flushes of primroses, clusters of the plants thick with perfumed flowers in every sheltered depression. Indeed, I do not remember ever seeing so many primroses in one day. The views were quite wonderful from this height, something over 300m above sea level; Slieve Elva, County Clare's highest point, was clear to the west, while to the east we were high enough to see the Shannon basin extending eastwards beyond

the Slieve Aughty Mountains. To the south were the great
swirling whale-backs of the bare Burren hills rising from a sea
of grey and green, while in the far distance lakes glittered. The
only features on the plateau besides the walls that crossed it
were occasional mohars, or stone-built sheep shelters, and a
number of curious rectangles of limestone flags about 1.5m
wide and 5m long, open at one end. Dick and I had come
across these before and had wondered at their origin.
Subsequently an old man had told Dick they were for collecting cowdung. We mused about what the cowdung was used
for and a light-hearted and far-reaching discussion followed
with much laughter. One possibility was that it was dried to
use as fuel for the evening fires of youngsters who looked after
the cattle during the booleying time in the summer, when live-
stock was taken onto pastures on high ground.

A walk of about 1km brought us to the northern end of
the plateau which is marked by the great cairn from which
the hill gets its name, although this is only one of a number
of Burren hills with such a prehistoric cairn. Another one,
which we would pass by later, was now in plain view a few
kilometres away at the western end of Turlough Hill. Across
the shapely eastern end of the hill the blue waters of Galway
Bay were in sight, Island Eddy in the middle, and beyond the
low-lying coast Lough Corrib could be identified, while on
the horizon nearly 70 miles to the north, Jenny picked out the
rounded lone profile of Nephin, at the foot of which was her
home. Away to the northwest the serrated outline of the
Twelve Bens could be vaguely made out against a hazy sky.
Two weeks previously I had climbed to the top of the highest
of them, Benbaun, from where Black Head and the Burren
coast were in clear view. From the same summit I could see
Mount Brandon 160km to the south, and the same Nephin

to the northeast, so I held a vast area of Ireland under my gaze. Ireland is a wonderfully small place, of a size and scale that can only easily be appreciated from its high places. The phrase 'the world is at your feet' well sums up the sensation of the summits.

I sat a while as the others went on ahead, thinking that the last place on my walk across Ireland that I had felt this level of euphoria was when crossing the Dublin Mountains; interesting and wild and lonely as the flat midlands had been, they did not seem to stir up the same emotions I felt on the higher altitudes.

I caught up with the others and we descended towards the saddle between Carran and Turlough, raising a large hare who must have stayed still crouching in the grass until we were right upon him, and only then bounding long-legged away, until he was out of sight. On the Slieve Carran side of the saddle we came across a spectacular limestone formation, a great circular amphitheatre carved out of the edge of the plateau, 300m across, its flat bottom 15m below us a sea of primroses, from which rose a couple of what looked like ruined structures. It actually appears on the ordnance map as two tiny contour lines in an oval shape. We sat down nearby and had a leisurely snack before continuing.

We negotiated a couple of cliffs to reach the saddle and followed a wall, which according to the map was also the boundary of County Galway, up onto Turlough Hill. The valley stretching westwards between the two hills was glorious to see from this angle, its bright green bottom overlooked by long, smooth and perfect limestone terraces that could have been a gigantic man-made stadium. The Burren has something of interest and many surprises at both the macro and the micro scale, from this vast geological wonder to the myriad herbs at our feet.

Near the top of Turlough Hill we encountered a low bank which enclosed a large area of ground on the crown of the hill, the remains of a hillfort, possibly of Iron Age date. Although it comprised a substantial area, it was unlikely that it was a 'fort' in the military sense; Dick felt that at best it may have been a religious site, or was used for something as mundane as an animal enclosure. We turned west now and climbed gently towards the cairn on the western tip of Turlough, passing by a short time later the remains of another prehistoric site, this time a small city of hut sites. Each consisted of a circle of stones, probably a little less than 10m across, the interior about half a metre below ground level, and some of them had extensions so that they looked on plan like the figure eight. The superstructure would probably have been of timber, and skins or thatch, possibly resembling an American Indian teepee. I counted about 23 of these sites, an amazing gathering of what might have been, I suppose, neolithic houses.

Great views to the north west were opening up ahead now, of Connemara extending out into the Atlantic, backed by the serrated shapes of the Twelve Bens and the Maum Turks. Below us to the north the grey ruins of Corcomroe Abbey stood out against a background of green fields. It was founded by the Cistercians, who were brought into this part of Clare around 1180, an interesting time for Ireland, by Donal More O'Brien, to develop the local land and sea resources. At the north wall of the chancel of the church is the tomb of the grandson of Donal More, Conor Siudaine O'Brien; he was buried there more than 700 years ago.

Mary pointed out that the fields near the abbey were, for the Burren, uncharacteristically organised, all running downhill in a north-south direction. Those near the abbey were particularly long and narrow, like rundale strips, and we had a lot of fun discussing Mary's theory that today's field pattern still reflected the monastic farm of the seventeenth century; I thought she might be right but Dick was not convinced.

At the western end of the ridge we climbed to the cairn, which was of a type I have not seen elsewhere in Ireland. It was shaped like a shallow pork pie, with the cairn proper sitting on top of and retained by a partially collapsed circular stone wall 1.8m high. Here we took a break again, sitting in the soft grass and eating our last supplies while we chatted about the remains of so many epochs of Irish history we had come across during the past few hours.

We dropped down diagonally towards the ruins at Oughtmama along a series of low cliffs of razor sharp, unforgiving, brittle limestone bedrock and loose scree. At this stage of the day, when we were all a little tired, there was always a danger of losing concentration and twisting or even breaking an ankle, so we all took our time. As the ground levelled out we cast about, looking for a way through a belt of thick, thorny scrub to reach the churches. Mary finally succeeded in finding a prickly tunnel through the hazel into a tree-shaded grassy enclosure in which stood the well-preserved ruins of two fine early Christian churches.

Little is known about Oughtmama except that it was once quite a large, well-populated place. Traces of a number of houses have been found, as well as evidence of a monastic enclosure wall, terraced gardens and a canal-fed water mill. The walls of the two churches are constructed of massive stones and the cut-stone work is exquisite, particularly the round-arched windows with deeply splayed reveals, which must have been a geometric nightmare to get right. The quoinstones, above the level where cattle have been polishing them by scratching themselves for ten centuries, are as sharp as the day they were made. I had visited Oughtmama a few times previously, and have always been struck by the special quality of the place, and this visit was no exception.

My watch told me it was 4.15pm, around the time I had originally suggested we might be back at Ballyvaghan, so against all my inclinations I felt we should drag ourselves away, so we struck out across a couple of boggy fields for the track which would take us down to the public road.

The trek along the tarmac was an uncomfortable contrasting interlude in what had been a great day. We were all a little tired now, and the heat of the afternoon had built up, but Mary and Jenny seemed to be in great spirits and there was much wit, repartee and laughter as we proceeded. Dick particularly impressed me; although he was someone who enjoyed the outdoors, he was not a regular walker, yet he was the life and soul of the party, and never complained of being footsore. The soles of my own feet, particularly the pads of my toes, were certainly sore, and telling me that they hated tarmac. When we began to run out of water, Jenny went into a farmhouse and returned with a fresh, blissfully cold supply to fill our bottles.

Soon after we were pleased to be able to turn off the main road and head again towards high ground, up a gravelly side road. Only one unknown remained; the route I had planned involved linking up two tracks shown on the Korff and O'Donnell map of the Burren, one which terminated on the east side of the low range which separated us from Ballyvaghan, and the other which came to an end on the west side. Success depended on being able to negotiate the terrain of what may have been, in the past, a pass between Ailwee and Moneen Mountains, at about 160m.

The road we were following eventually ended at a gate giving access to the farmyard of a very remote farmhouse. At this stage the only alternative route was to backtrack to near Corcomroe and walk by road to Ballyvaghan, a distance of probably 12km, so we were going to have to persuade the farmer we needed to pass through. Mary and I volunteered, and we opened the squeaking gate and went in, expecting to be immediately met by dogs. There were none, however, and we knocked on the farmhouse door. A middle-aged man, who looked as if he lived alone, came to the door.

'Would it be alright if we walked on up the track? We want to get to Ballyvaghan,' inquired Mary.

He said nothing for a moment as he looked us up and down; I'm sure he had few calling at the door, and even less asking for permission to cross his land.

'Oh ye can,' he said. 'There's a car gone up ahead of ye.'

We didn't know what he meant by this, but with great relief we thanked him profusely, and went back to get the others.

We ascended the steep track which zig-zagged towards the skyline, while Mary and Jenny discussed the fate of Irish farmers in isolated places, and the difficulty of getting a wife to join them. We gained altitude quickly, while a great view opened up behind of the green valley between Turlough and Gortaclare, the western extension of Carran, from which we had looked down from the opposite direction a few hours before. The track continued southwards as it reached a level just under the ridge; the car he mentioned must have gone up there but we saw no sign of it. At this point we were less than 100m below the ridge so we turned uphill across karst pavements once again into a breeze from the west we had not felt all day. We were slower now, a little weary maybe, as we

negotiated the giant steps in the limestone, but having crossed a wall just under the brow of the ridge we found ourselves on yet another broad stoney plateau, with a new horizon of Burren landscape ahead to the west. I was anxious at this stage, having dragged these good people up and down hill all day, to assure myself that what remained of the route I had planned was viable, and I hurried ahead into the breeze across a sea of waving mountain avens to reach the western side of the plateau.

It was a considerable relief to finally see, not too far away, my ultimate goal, the village of Ballyvaghan nestling at the edge of Galway Bay. The great massif of Black Head and Gleninagh Mountain towered over it, and away across the bay the Twelve Bens were more sharply defined now against the evening sky. Below about 1km away I made out the track we should be heading for, and traced its meandering course into Ballyvaghan. I was full of delight, and tired no longer, as for the last time that day, we scrambled down a series of low limestone cliffs and descended into a wild valley overlooked by two stone forts, one of which must have given the townsland to the west its name, Dangan, which means fortress. It was 6.45pm, and before we left the pavements behind we gathered at a large boulder, and lit up by the gold evening sun, by taking a group photograph. As she had been at Oughtmama, Mary was successful in finding a route through the ubiquitous hazel scrub cordon that separated us from the road, and by 7.15pm, after one short detour when I led the others in the opposite direction by mistake, we were walking into Ballyvaghan.

Jenny and Mary, hardy souls, left almost immediately to return to Mayo where Jenny's son was awaiting the loan of her car to go out for the night. Dick and I, after a shower, just managed to make last serving in a small restaurant where we tucked into a steak dinner, washed down with a couple of pints; heaven on earth! It was very pleasant, but as always at the end of long treks, a sense of regret was woven through my sense of achievement regret that it was over. Shortly after we had returned to our guesthouse for the night and turned in, I got up again and, putting on some clothes, wandered outside and across the road, to where I could see the twinkling lights of the coast of Galway across the bay. It was cool and the air was clean and perfumed with night-scented shrub. I stood a while running over in my mind the Ireland I had seen and the people I had met, and the joy of being for a few short periods anyway, a tramp, without a care in the world. What next, I asked myself, and returned to my bed and a good night's sleep.

GALWAY COUNTY LIBRARIES

Epilogue

Since this last crossing of Ireland a number of other possibilities for improvement of the route have become apparent. For instance, there is a possibility of using a section of the East Clare Way as an alternative to those roads west of Portumna, and there may be a chance to vary the Grand Canal section by using at least a section of the Brosna. Although I had failed twice to make some use out of the old Clara to Banagher railway line, I am still convinced that there are possibilities here too.

There can be no doubt that readers local to some of the areas mentioned will be asking themselves 'how did he miss' this or that possibility? I would be very grateful if they would let me know if I have so missed an opportunity in their area.

To walk from our eastern shores to the Atlantic is a great way to experience Ireland, and although more work will be required before the route can be finalised satisfactorily, I would like to see it becoming, before too long, a fully approved Irish Waymarked Trail.

Index of Places

GALWAY COUNTY LIBRARIES